Desire

Desire

in seven voices

Edited by

LORNA CROZIER

Douglas & McIntyre

Vancouver/Toronto

99 00 01 02 03 5 4 3 2 1

Douglas & McIntyre Ltd.
2323 Quebec Street, Suite 201
Vancouver, British Columbia
V5T 4S7

CANADIAN CATALOGUING IN PUBLICATION DATA

Main entry under title:
Desire in seven voices

   ISBN 1-55054-738-0

   1. Desire—Literary collections. 2. Canadian essays (English)—Women
authors. 3. Canadian essays (English)—20th century.*
I. Crozier, Lorna, 1948–
PS8367.D47D47 1999   C814'.5408'03538   C99-910602-3
PR9197.7.D47 1999

Editing by Barbara Pulling
Jacket and text design by Val Speidel
Jacket photograph by Brenda Hemsing
Printed and bound in Canada by Friesens
Printed on acid-free paper ∞

Canadä

The publisher gratefully acknowledges the support of the Canada Council for the
Arts and of the British Columbia Ministry of Tourism, Small Business and Culture.
The publisher also acknowledges the financial support of the Government of
Canada through the Book Publishing Industry Development Program.

In memory of Leslie Ashcroft,
who so valued the company of women

and for Louise Leclair

my friends, my sweet barbarians,
there is that hunger which is not for food—

. . .

let us make an anthology of recipes,
let us edit for breakfast
our most unspeakable appetites—

GWENDOLYN MACEWEN
"A Breakfast for Barbarians"

CONTENTS

INTRODUCTION:
DESIRE IN SEVEN VOICES

Lorna Crozier

S EVEN: A NUMBER OF MAGIC and wisdom in the female realm. Multiplied by the moon's four phases, it becomes twenty-eight, the approximate number of days in the lunar month and the menstrual cycle. The dim stars in the cluster Pleiades have been variously called the Seven Sisters, the Seven Mothers of the World and the Seven Sages. According to a mediaeval superstition, a group of seven women was a source of fear and trepidation: one of them was sure to be a vampire or a werewolf. Suffice it to say, wherever seven women appear together, the air is charged. There is something disturbing, something vibrant going on.

The Muses, those classical goddesses of inspiration, invented the seven-tone musical scale based on the harmonies of the heavenly spheres. Seven, then, is also the number of the muses' melodies, of breath and the stroking of strings transformed into song. Here, in highly original and personal essays that are making their first appearance in print, seven female voices in as many tones explore the contemporary and earthly realms of desire.

Each of the writers was asked to consider the following questions: "When do you trust your desire? When do you censor it? When is it a source of power, and when a source of distress?" We entered the territory warily, our senses on full alert. Desire is, after all, an intimate thing, a sensation often nurtured in privacy and clandestine fantasy. For many, its natural language is reticence; it communicates through glance and gesture. Even close friends who talk about almost everything else with honesty, ribaldry and compassion may rarely discuss desire. It remains one of the last taboos, perhaps more so than eroticism, for desire usually includes an element of loss. Its very articulation extinguishes the fire that was part of the original, seductive craving.

I knew this collection was going to be remarkable when I wrestled with the topic like Jacob with his angel until my thigh was wounded, and when my fellow writers—all highly accomplished and experienced in their craft—described the same kind of struggle. The difficulty the seven of us had in finding words for what has been unspoken is surely a sign of a tremendous force building to a breaking point just below the surface. When desire finds expression in the voices of such writers as these, its resistance to words, its own stubborn desire to remain subterranean creates a complexity and an energy that suffuses every sentence.

In Carol Shields' fictionalized essay, the central character recalls a vacation she and her then-husband spent in Paris. Their hotel was built around an air shaft, the windows of the rooms facing each other. One morning, from one of the open windows, they heard a woman's orgasmic cry. I like to think of these seven essays facing each other between the covers of this book, their variegated sounds funnelling into a tall airy space, their separate stories of love and longing weaving in and out, the musical notes—tender and familiar or violent and sad—rising and falling, touching every place desire can dwell.

Desire

JUNKIE LIBIDO

Susan Musgrave

JUNKIE LIBIDO

m u s g r a v e

AT THE AGE OF FOURTEEN I found my virginity. No sacred spring gushed forth to mark the spot, though years later the University of Victoria erected its Faculty of Law where my blood had stained the grass.

I had to lose it to discover what it was. We'd touched on "nocturnal emissions" in Guidance (boys had them in their dreams; girls didn't), and skimmed the vulva, the vagina and other woman-parts our counsellor suggested we might one day stumble upon "down there." Labia minora sounded like a Mediterranean island. I don't think the clitoris, the word or the elusive organ, was in any kind of usage back then.

Our counsellor told us, too, that girls were supposed to "save themselves" for the right man. I couldn't wait. After my brown-eyed boy wormed, poked, prodded, stabbed, tore, ripped, thrust and otherwise negotiated his way inside the place I didn't know I had, he called my name. I knew he didn't expect me to answer: some things you know, and the rest you learn by finding out. Later, after apologizing for what he'd done, he kissed me and bicycled home. Alone under the budding trees I reached between my thighs to feel where our wetness had dried, tight and shiny like a scar.

The next afternoon, in an old boathouse smelling of high tide, fish and water rats, he taught me how to light a banana slug on fire, how to make it melt into a pool of sticky ooze. Then he undid his zipper and pulled out his penis, and I thought for a terrible moment he wanted me to light *it* on fire, to even the score for what he had done to me in the woods. Instead he said, "Put your mouth on it," and when I did it grew thicker and harder until I felt my

Susan Musgrave

mouth fill with a hot gush of thick, salty fluid. I thought I'd
cut him with my tooth, the crooked one my parents could
never afford to have straightened. His penis started shrink-
ing right away; I thought I must have a mouthful of his
blood. I had split him open and drained him and now he
was shrivelling like the unlucky banana slug. I wanted to
spit, but, having been brought up properly, I swallowed my
mouthful instead. I figured now we'd have to hitch a ride to
Emergency and wondered how I was going to explain the
presence of my mouth in a boy's private region, let alone
cutting and draining him and swallowing the evidence.

"I've cut you," I said. "I think I hit an artery."

Then he said, his fucky brown eyes more open to me
than ever, "That wasn't blood, sweetheart."

All spring and summer long we consumed each other,
making love in forests and in fields, in broom closets, on
chesterfields in rich peoples' houses where I babysat, in
spring rain, on railway tracks, in Chinatown back alleys, on
mossy rocks smelling of wild onions, up against the
perimeter fence surrounding our junior high school after
reading bedroom scenes torn from Henry Miller's *Sexus*.
When I had my first orgasm I thought sex had driven me

insane, that I was going to drown in the rogue wave of terrible pleasure that rolled over my body and pulled me down in a libidinous undertow. I didn't care. Sex was worth dying for, not just once but over and over. For a feeling this completely sweet and sad and good it was worth spending the rest of my life locked up in a mental hospital.

But with desire came loss, and fear: loss of innocence and fear that the pleasure would have to end. My best friend's mother had told her she would get cancer if she let a boy touch her breasts. It wouldn't happen immediately; it might take years for the cells to begin multiplying all out of control. I had let a boy do a lot more than get to first base, and when I missed my period, I decided I must be terminally ill.

I spent hours in my bedroom composing odes to myself, trying to come up with some pithy epitaph for my headstone, one my friends would forever remember me by, like ALWAYS. Back then ALWAYS wasn't the brand name of a female sanitary product. No odour-free panty liner would come between my white cotton panties and the hot, earthy, ocean-ripe smell of my pent-up juices and desires.

When "the curse" came, a full day later than usual, my boy and I made love again, in a graveyard, under a lukewarm

S u s a n   M u s g r a v e

sun. Part of me, I promised, would always belong to him. But even as I spoke, in my heart I felt a hot, secret tugging to be somewhere else.

My parents were pleased. They felt a girl my age should be dating all kinds of different boys, especially the type they approved of, who played rugby and called my father "Sir," the ones from well-to-do families who would grow up and demand to be called "Sir" themselves by wives they chained to the kitchen sink trap while they made furtive love to fourteen-year-olds like me.

These well-bred boys always respected me too much to go all the way. They respected, that is, the boundaries they had drawn to protect themselves, which meant no cheap excursions to Labia minora or other foreign parts requiring, in their minds, the passport of marriage, or at least a temporary entry visa. But after sucking my nipples until I was ready to fuck the stick shift out of their old man's BMW, they drove me home and made me beg to be allowed to blow them in the driveway. *Please, Sir, can I have some more?*

Because I desired, I made myself desirable, wearing what I perceived to be the trappings—see-through blouses, black leather boots that reached for my thighs, a miniskirt the size of a heating pad my mother said "left nothing to the imagination." She, on the other hand, could imagine everything, especially the worst. Freedom did not mean the freedom to become anything I chose, she said, meaning a nymphomaniac—what girls who *enjoyed* sex were called in those days, girls with normal healthy appetites by today's standards. (The "maniac" part I could live up to, but "nympho" made me sound like the town pump.) To cool my desires my parents shipped me off to California to spend the summer sun-worshipping with my wealthy godmother, who lived alone in an isolated ranchette in gold-rush country in the hills above Sacramento.

My rehabilitation was cut short when my godmother caught me sunbathing beneath a blond, blue-eyed California surfer who'd come home to the hills to pump gas for the summer; she sent me and my sunscreen packing, saying I had a mind of my own and was clearly oversexed. I needed help with both these tragedies, everyone seemed to think. My parents had me committed to a mental hospital.

The kindred spirits I met there called the institution the "Garden of Eden," because even in this healing environment

Susan Musgrave

of group and shock therapy, sex was everybody's downfall. The apple of my eye was a thirty-eight-year-old absent-minded professor from California, who lost his job when my parents threatened to have him charged with statutory rape. We fled to Berkeley—leaving behind his wife and four kids under six—escaping from the mental hospital by exiting through a door marked ENTRANCE ONLY. "Who will ever marry her now?" my Victorian father said.

He needn't have worried: my desire was never for marriage. Desire was two bodies banging together in the dark, leaping from a burning plane without a parachute, diving into the wreckage of ourselves and finding parts of our bodies no one had ever discovered or named, reinventing the future. I desired only, and always, to be desired.

I stayed with my professor until I felt it again—that hot, secret tugging to be somewhere else. Back home, in the country where I belonged, I found someone new. After this new someone came another, and another. As I grew older, I became less and less discriminating. I was an attraction addict, and when you need a quick fix, you stop being choosy. I no longer believed there was any part of me left to save for any man, even the wrong one. Falling in love became the gauze I applied over the wet wound of the heart, and love, my heart-stopper drug. When romance started to look iffy, and passion turned to depression and despair, I would begin my search all over again. Any man was the right man as long as he could jump-start my junkie libido.

There is, of course, a scientific explanation for this emotional disturbance we call desire. Some experts maintain that we "fall in love" when the neurons in our limbic system, our emotional core, become saturated by a small molecule called phenyl-ethylamine, or PEA, and other naturally occurring amphetamines. High on this organic brain "speed," lovers stay awake all night talking about the future, reliving the past, falling in giddy love with each other, and with themselves, over and over again. The slightest thought of your sweetheart—a letter in the mail, a phone message, the mention of his name—sends a tsunami of exhilaration through your brain. You quit eating, lose weight, get pimples (I *know* it's true love when my face breaks out). The hermit you always thought you were wakes up each day delirious, gregarious, in an optimistic, euphoric, stuttering, agonizing, blissful, *adjectivey* state. Love, we say, is to die for. As if there can be nothing better, nothing hotter or holier on this earth.

It would be too simple to say that desire—this neural itch, this alert, intoxicating, deep, mystical devotion to another human being—is due solely to natural stimulants in the brain. But understanding what made me so strung out leaves me these days feeling less like a prisoner of my desire than a hostage with enough information to negotiate my way through a neurochemical jungle. For if desire is what happens when you're flying on natural speed, brain chemistry can be held responsible for the end of the affair, also. Either the brain endings adapt and are no longer affected by the onslaught of amphetamines, or the levels of PEA begin to drop. The brain can't go on forever in this heightened state of etherized romantic bliss. Your brain wants to get you off one kind of drug—and onto another.

As the excitement and novelty subside (anywhere between eighteen months and three years after attraction begins), a natural morphine-like substance kicks in that calms the mind. As these endorphins surge through the brain they usher in the second phase of love—attachment, bringing with it the sensations of security and peace. But if you're like I used to be, craving the constant high induced by insecurity and war, and not yet ready for morphine-surrender, the cool dependable fires of attachment, you'll do what I did over and over again: break the bonds of love and abandon the idea of becoming permanently attached to anyone.

My first marriage began to crumble around the time I developed the habit of dipping graham wafers in my morning cup of tea. (Perhaps it was a coincidence, but as Jung said, if traced back far enough, coincidence becomes inevitable.) After being dunked in the cup that cheers but does not inebriate, the crackers get mushy and can be swallowed without being masticated. We drink liquids and we chew solids, but I've never found a word for the way tea-infused graham wafers are ingested.

In the early days of my first marriage I permitted myself only four graham wafers each morning with my first cup of tea; later, when my husband began to obsess about my compulsive behaviour, I stopped counting. By then I'd noticed, too, a change in my libido.

With a little research it has been easy to find out where my favourite tea, the Iron Goddess of Mercy, is grown—on the slopes of Amoy, China, where it is harvested by specially trained monkeys. Graham wafers were invented in the early 1800s by Sylvester Graham, who served them to children in his boarding house because he believed it stopped them from abusing themselves. But does anyone really know where the libido comes from? The *Gage Canadian* says its origin is the Latin *libido*, meaning desire, but that's the *word*, not the thing: the thing that appears out of nowhere, rising and floating, lighter than air.

When I learned about Sylvester Graham's motives in dishing out wafers to his wards (as a child, I too had pleasured myself by immersing graham wafers in my Bunnikins mug full of milk), I began to suspect the soggy biscuits might have something to do with the decline and fall of my own sexual urges. But even this knowledge didn't stop me. I craved more and more. Some mornings I ate so many graham wafers I wasn't able to force down the breakfast my good-hearted husband had laid out for me.

My husband was a criminal lawyer defending five Americans and eighteen Colombians charged with smuggling thirty tonnes of marijuana into Canada. When they'd run out of rolling papers, they'd brought their ship in for supplies on the west coast of Vancouver Island. The same day I ate an entire box of graham wafers, dunking each straight into the pot without taking the trouble to pour myself a cup of tea first, the jury acquitted the smugglers, and one of them, the future father of my child, walked out of the courthouse wearing an unbleached linen suit and a T-shirt that said "I SCORED."

I offered him a ride. To South America, or as far as we could get. I was ready to give up my graham wafer habit and start afresh, I said. On the steps of the courthouse I looked at him and saw, in the gleam of his own shadowy eyes, a depth of wanting that promised heaven. It wasn't until years later I realized that the desire must have been my own reflected back, that the promise I thought I saw had been nothing more than the neglected spirit of my own lust.

I knew little about this stranger I so adventitiously desired, and I liked it that way: mystery and unknowing are energy. We spent two weeks camping in the Gulf Islands in the rain; under cover of false ID we crossed the border into

Washington State. In Sudden Valley we camped by a fire and drank white rum and Paul showed me his tattoo—a pair of faded lips, as if a ghost wearing lipstick had kissed him above his left nipple. We kept each other warm until the nights turned cold, then flew the Whisperliner Jet Service to Miami, and from there to Central America, where we rented post office boxes in four countries. When my great-aunt in England wrote that she was "puzzled by our freedom of choice for place of domicile, which is usually determined by the husband's place of work," I didn't have the heart to tell her Paul wasn't my husband.

After a year we rented an apartment in Panama City. We had a view of the ocean, and of the freighters lined up waiting to enter the Canal. When Paul's work, his *negocios delicados*, took him south to Colombia and Bolivia, I spent my days writing erotic poetry in a walled garden filled with orange-blossoming trees, vines that dripped a lavender-scented moss, and bougainvillea. To make up for having stayed away so long, Paul always came back with souvenirs he'd bought for me in airport gift shops: a silver llama brooch, a Peruvian devil-dancer, coca leaves for me to chew to replace my graham wafer cravings. But each time he stayed away a little longer, and I decided I would have to explore Panama City on my own.

I enrolled in Spanish lessons at the YMCA in the Canal Zone and took a taxi there each morning to learn "useful phrases of everyday life" such as, "My wife plays the piano very well," and "Do you expect me to cart around that miserable little last year's hat?" One taxi driver, his face like polished black hardwood, took me the long way home, into the *olla*, the slums, where he unzipped his trousers, using sign language to demonstrate his desire to join me in the back seat of his cab. I asked him, in my new Spanish, if he expected me to wear that miserable little last year's hat while my wife played the piano? He looked at me in the rear-view mirror, trying to decide whether I was a maniac or a nympho. He must have settled on the former, because he drove me straight home without further deviation.

Whenever I asked Paul why I couldn't join him in Colombia, he told me it was too dangerous. As a *gringa* I would be an obvious target for kidnappers. Colombia remained too dangerous for me right up until the day I discovered a sharp red fingernail clipping in one of his trouser pockets. Then he confessed. The danger was Elizabeth.

He described her, over the phone: how her hands felt hot to the touch (he complained that mine were always cold), how she was "something of a poet herself" and had won a prize in high school. That night I packed and booked a flight to Vancouver. But Paul got back before my plane left the ground and told me, over "Mired Seafood" at La Casa de Mariscos, that he was trying hard not to fall in love with Elizabeth. I wanted to say this was fair, we had never promised each other everlasting love, but my heart shrivelled into a fist and I stabbed him with my fork instead.

"I wish you could meet the person who causes you so much unhappiness," Paul said, when he eventually stopped bleeding.

Elizabeth was not the femme fatale I'd pictured—tall, full of sophisticated talk about punting in Brazil, cigarette smouldering in an ivory holder. The day we met she wore a Snoopy watch and chewed gum non-stop, and even in red stilettos she was always the last one to know it was raining.

When Paul and I had settled into the penthouse he'd rented for us in Cali, in southern Colombia, I invited

Elizabeth for dinner. She asked to read some of my poetry and, to be polite, I asked her what *she* did for a living. She was employed by MAS, she said. I assumed this must be the Colombian equivalent of the Rotary Club, a group committed to doing good work for the community, until she told me MAS stood for *Muerte a Secuestradores*—literally "Death to Kidnappers"—and her current job involved smuggling grenades—in her vagina—into local prisons and blowing up notorious *secuestradores*. She spoke as casually about killing people as Paul now constantly spoke of his desire for me to have his child.

When the time came for Paul to travel again, I helped him pack. I drove him to the airport in his linen suit and the T-shirt he always wore when he was leaving me, but the words "I SCORED" had faded in the sun and were almost unreadable.

Psychopharmacologists argue that the motivation to achieve an altered mood or consciousness is a "fourth drive," as much a part of the human condition, and as important to most other species, as sex, thirst and hunger. During the Vietnam War water buffalo were observed nibbling on opium poppies more often than they do in times of peace, the same way the American soldiers, fighting the Viet Cong, took to using heroin. From caffeine and graham wafers to marijuana and heroin, most of us use drugs for one purpose: to change our mood, to medicate ourselves when we feel overburdened by the enormous tragedies of late twentieth-century life.

I remember a dinner party on Vancouver Island, back in the mid-seventies, where our host passed round a human skull before dessert, collecting donations for a gram of coke, a six-pack, a bottle of tequila—whatever he could score out there in the world of the living. Later, when we had all scooped a couple of grams of glitter into the drains of our waiting nostrils, I sat on the beach in front of the house with my friend Tom York, who abstained from substances, and who talked about his desire for "desirelessness." Tom, who'd moved from Arkansas to the B.C. wilderness during the Vietnam War, was a United Church minister who read Heidegger before breakfast, a writer who killed and ate a bear for his fortieth birthday, a weightlifter who could dead-lift three hundred pounds, a marathon runner, a philan-derer—when anyone accused him of being immoral in his pursuits of the flesh, he reminded them not to confuse religion with morality—and a gentleman. The last time I saw him, before he was killed on an interstate highway, he played Percy Sledge singing "When a Man Loves a Woman" for me in Waterloo, Ontario. Tom used to say I was unique among the women he knew, because I had never desired him in the ways a woman most often desires a man. Flattery was Tom's Southern way of engaging in social intercourse.

Back then I argued: to be desireless was to be dead. Tom just listened and nodded his head and drew on the pipe he smoked. I said I couldn't remember a time when desire wasn't wailing in my veins, wetting the insides of my thighs all the way up into the Bermuda Triangle between my legs where all men, and love, eventually disappeared. Then I would begin my quest again, running up long-distance phone bills, changing continents as often as I changed my underwear, my phone number, my address, my eating habits, my sleeping patterns. Desire kept me in the wind and on fire, burning wild, out of control, and in need of a search party to find my own self after a night in bed with some—in retrospect—wholly insignificant other.

S u s a n   M u s g r a v e

Tom's novel of New Orleans, *Desireless*, was published posthumously. I know now that Tom wasn't talking only about sexual desire, though his wife had named thirty-nine co-respondents when she'd petitioned for a divorce. I wish he were still alive so we could laugh about my naïveté. How long and hard I argued about something Tom (not to mention the Buddhists, and Freud) had always understood: that desire is the cause of all suffering, that we are never so defenceless against suffering as when we love.

I had promised my first love a part of me would always be his. A part of me has kept that promise. Some nights I dream of my brown-eyed boy, of our last time together in the long grass in the graveyard, where we thought lust made us invisible. When he opens his eyes I am gone, and on the headstone that was our pillow, my epitaph: "Behold, Desire!"

FATHER FIGURES

Evelyn Lau

FATHER FIGURES

Lau

DISTANCE, FOR ME, kindles desire. When I was growing up it was my crushes on the teachers that preoccupied me, not the freckle-faced boy's fumbling kiss behind the bushes at recess. Not what was close and possible. It was these older men with their mysterious lives whom I invested with the power of protecting me.

It has always been this way, and sometimes I think it always will. At almost any given time I will have a crush on a man who is somehow impossible. The word "crush" is appropriate, because the feeling is entirely adolescent in its short-lived intensity. The object of my distant affections is likely someone I have met only a few times, someone who displays no interest in me. He has no inkling of the feelings I have for him; quite possibly he would be startled and embarrassed if he knew. I never express my interest, since if he responded that would instantly end my infatuation. If he is married, he will have shown himself as the sort of married man who has affairs and who is therefore untrustworthy. If he isn't married, his availability alone would send me running. Besides, if I actually got to know him better I would have to acknowledge that his real personality bears no resemblance to the inordinately loving and attentive one I give him in my thoughts.

Although these crushes are not without some of the heartache of unrequited love, I do enjoy them, in a way. They are innocent, uncomplicated by sex, or spending the night, or the daily challenges of a relationship. They are curiously pure; my imagination rarely indulges in anything more intimate than kissing and cuddling. As I write this, I am nursing a crush on a middle-aged married man. He is successful and energetic, obsessed with his work; he wears conservative suits and has the face of someone's rich uncle. I met him twice and will probably never see him again. This is fine by me, since I try so hard to conceal my interest that I am awkward and speechless around him. I would welcome his presence in my life, but the sensations he stirs in me make friendship impossible. At the same time, only by getting to know him better, understanding who he is independently of my fantasy, could I put him into human perspective and end my infatuation.

When I look back over the past decade, I am dismayed by how often desire, or even the perceived threat of desire—a man's or mine—has prevented the inclusion in my life of some interesting, even brilliant men. A wife's groundless jealousy in situations where no attraction exists, a man's confessed infatuation, a drunken kiss one regrettable night—each is enough to create a permanent rift.

Desire, for me, is often strangely divorced from sex. What I most desire—an entrance into another's life, the sudden flare of emotional contact, intellectual stimulation—is not compelled by a sexual motive. But this sort of desire can be as powerful an urge as sex. I once had an intense emotional connection with a married man that never went near sex, yet this so threatened his wife that it contributed to the end of their marriage. How could she believe that the most risqué fantasy I had of us was that I might put my head on his shoulder, breathe in his comforting, paternal smell, and go to sleep? How could she believe that the driving force of my life has been to find a man who would look at me as though I were his daughter?

My own father adored me when I was a child. It appeared I was the centre of his universe; when we played together my reflection danced in the lenses of his glasses, as if I were all that filled his vision. I loved him passionately and would spend long nights agonizing about losing him—he would be attacked on the street on his way home from work, he would sicken and die, my mother would force him to leave. His safety was paramount in my mind, so that my mother's interference in the capsule of our love was not merely an inconvenience to me but a real threat—when he finished my bedtime story and proceeded down the hall to the bedroom he shared with his wife, I would lie awake gripped with fear, certain that she was waiting in the darkness to injure him.

To lose my father would be to lose not only love and attention but the shield between myself and my mother, whom I saw as a frightening force in the family, given to unpredictable rages and a need for humiliating dominance over me. I prayed nightly for his safety; he survived intact, but when I was nine years old my mother gave birth to another baby girl, and his attention flickered away from me. Then he lost his job, and our lives changed. He entered the world of his own misery, trudging home day after day from job interviews that led nowhere. He would disappear into the basement to send out more resumés and to do the contract work that provided our meagre income. My mother belittled him for being unemployed, and her anxiety over our financial future aggravated her compulsive behaviour. Desperate to escape my mother's control, murderously jealous of my new sibling, bewildered by the withdrawal of my father's affection, I became obsessed with writing and the fantasy life it afforded. At school I was an outcast, and the combination of my classmates' merciless teasing and my unhappiness at home meant I spent most nights praying I would die in my sleep. To comfort myself, I began bingeing in secret, which led to constant mockery from my mother and an embarrassed averting of my father's gaze from my growing chubbiness. Depressed, nearly suicidal, I would sit in my room gorging on hoarded food while my parents went shopping on weekends. It seemed to me then that everything had already been lost.

At fourteen, I ran away from the life I could no longer endure. I left the father I could no longer look at without pain clouding my vision and stood on street corners so other fathers could pay attention to me for the time it took to give them an orgasm. Prostitution was my introduction to sex; inevitably, it confused my understanding of desire and inhibited my interest in my own sexuality. I learned to regard desire as something that resided, raging, only in men. Often the sex I had with clients was so repugnant and physically uncomfortable I took to swallowing painkillers beforehand, in order to feel as little as possible. It took years to emerge from that period of my life, with all its self-destructive behaviour, and when I did I actually thought I might never have sex again, though its darker permutations fascinated me as a writer. Sex lent itself so readily to literary exploration of power, of loyalty and its absence, of boundaries tested.

Evelyn Lau

I was amazed when people would ask me questions like, "Just between us, didn't you ENJOY it when you were hooking?" How could they be so ignorant, particularly the women? But these were women who had had mostly positive sexual experiences, who praised the physical sensation of intercourse. They didn't seem to know what it was like to be so unwilling that it was painful to have a stranger's penis in you, or to be so numb and detached you felt absolutely nothing. They couldn't comprehend it because they hadn't lived it, just as when I was a teenager I couldn't understand why anyone would ever have sex unless she was being paid for it.

But when I was twenty years old I fell desperately in love with a married man who lived in another city, and for several years I drowned in the certainty that I had met the one person meant for me. He was a prominent executive, polished and urbane; privately, he was tormented. When we met, on a night rain ran into the gutters, I was stricken—the blaze of his eyes as we sat next to each other at the restaurant table, his skin as smooth as white stone. I was mesmerized by him in a way I never thought I could be. Later he said that when he drove home that night, thinking about me, he was shaking.

Our "affair" consisted of hotel room fumblings that never culminated in intercourse, and long conversations where we would cry because he wanted to be with me but could not bear to leave his marriage. He was really the first person I met that I wanted to be with, the first man with whom I was able to equate sex and love, physical desire and emotional desire. His childhood poverty, his father's physical abuse and his self-made success meant he had developed a wariness that mirrored my own, and a similar ability to make swift assessments of people's motivations. It took years for the pain of our impossible relationship to subside. Even after it became clear that he would never leave his wife, and that we must not continue seeing each other, I could not imagine going out on dates or sleeping with other men. I hated myself, thought if I were more attractive or confident he would have stayed with me. I know he is still living with his beautiful blonde wife. The gold band gleams on his finger. Even now, after a few drinks with friends, I sometimes like to say that if he were to walk in the door today and ask me to marry him, I would. Such is the effect, I suppose, of that first instance of looking at someone and wanting him entirely: his skin, his scent, his power and his vulnerability.

It was the first time I had seen physical beauty in a man, the first time I longed for someone with all my heart.

The entanglement with this man made me miserable. At times I thought I was losing my mind. There is a history of schizophrenia on my mother's side of the family—as a child, I worried that every imaginative thought I had, every period of depression or anxiety, heralded the advent of my own psychosis—and I grew up watching one of my aunts throw dishes against the wall during dinner, or start to scream because she saw the faces of men in the mirror ogling her when she stepped out of the shower. Periodically she would wander the streets and we would get a late-night phone call from the psychiatric ward, informing us she had been brought in by ambulance. When we visited her in the hospital she shuffled towards us in her fluffy slippers, looking small and embarrassed, apologizing to my parents for having again brought shame upon our family. My relatives chalked up her craziness to the scourge of unrequited love. It was said that the psychotic episodes began when she fell obsessively in love with her boss at work, who was married and had no interest in her. The sorrow of this had snapped something in her brain. It was a romantic notion without sound medical support, but during the worst of my own obsession, when there was clearly no chance for this man and me, it didn't appear so implausible. I never thought I could be so consumed by another person.

Now, I find it remarkable and a bit dismaying how rare it is for me to desire someone beyond a mild, entertaining crush. I meet men of all ages I like and admire, whose intellect and wit impress me, but I feel absolutely no attraction. I have gone on dates with men who fit the picture of what I typically find appealing, but without the least spark or surge of feeling. What is that thing that catches at your heart, seizes you, shakes you? What chemical reactions over which we have no command? I have many male friends and enjoy the company of men, but these relationships are platonic. I don't understand people whose friendships turn into sexual affairs, or vice versa; for me there is a strong line between a friendship and a sexual relationship. I regard it as almost morally wrong to confuse the two. My male friends talk to me openly about their involvements with women; if I were one of those women, they would cease to be so honest, and anyway I could not then bear that degree of truth. I prize

E v e l y n   L a u

honesty, despise the evasiveness and lies relationships seem to thrive on.

I wish I could write about plain, simple, lusty desire, the allure of another's heat and physical body uncomplicated by thought or rationale. I have felt that sort of desire, fleetingly, only two or three times in my life, for men who otherwise did not interest me. It confounded and terrified me; I did everything to protect myself from it. It took away the control I was able to maintain around men who did not much interest me sexually. Usually the men I find myself drawn to are not physically attractive—they tend to be establishment figures, middle-aged or older, grey-haired and intellectually formidable. They hold positions of some power in society. They may be paunchy or wrinkled, stooped or arthritic. They may have physical aspects that actually repel me. But it's their keen insight, their perceptive gaze that I find compelling; it's how observant they are, how well they understand people and their motivations. They possess qualities that are desirable to me, yet they are unable to weaken me with lust.

When I was a child my parents instilled in me the belief that because I was Chinese, and they were immigrants,

I would always be inferior to other Canadians; I would have to work twice as hard, be twice as respectable just to be accepted by this society. Their beliefs were reinforced by the occasional, always shocking, racial taunt in the schoolyard, on the bus, from a stranger passing on the street. What a powerful mix of longing and shame roiled in me! I always felt I was the outsider, pressing my face against the glass, craving to join those people fortunate enough to be in the light and the warmth. Perhaps that is partly why I was drawn from the beginning to men whose lives on the surface appeared unblemished and enviable; I wanted to be accepted by them, to find myself safe inside their houses.

I don't think I am capable of feeling desire without a complex of emotions and justifications—and that, some men might say, is just what is so unfair about the difference between women and men. For many women, it seems, and certainly for me, pure physical desire can go dormant for long periods of time, chased underground by anything from a traumatic end to a relationship to problems at work. A female friend once told me that in the years between

Evelyn Lau

relationships her sexual desire dwindled "to something the size of a pea, tucked way, way back in a corner of my mind." Yet when she is in a relationship that sexual urge is as alive as that of any man she is with.

I find myself writing this essay during a rather bleak period of my life. Desire is dim, pushed down and away. When I was twenty-four I finally ventured into another relationship, with an older writer. I have never been drawn to writers, since there is no mystery for me in what they do, no entry to an unknown world such as that a man in a different occupation would provide. But this man seemed harmless and unintimidated by my past. It ended badly, with him suing me over an article I wrote about our relationship. I had been hoping to make sense of my time with him, redeem something that felt merely painful and wasted. But for a year and a half the lawsuit continued to tie us together when I wanted to move forward in my life. I joked with friends that the situation finally taught me all about marriage and divorce, without me having to actually go through either.

I try to see the litigation as a learning experience, but I worry that it will leave a stain as permanent as the one left behind by years of prostitution. This man, thirty-six years older than I, had come closer than anyone to mirroring my relationship with my father; I saw him as a protector, and the lawsuit devastated me.

An acquaintance of mine, a stylish woman in her forties with a good career, was years ago financially ruined by her divorce from a high-flying entrepreneur. She remains flirtatious with men, almost girlish, but she is hard-hearted now. She rarely dates, and she speaks of men in a calculating way, in terms of what they can give her. She recognizes her need for sex as a nuisance that must be taken care of now and then; once or twice a year she goes on holiday, drinks too much and ends up in bed with a stranger, kicking him out the next morning without giving him her real name or her phone number. She refers to sex as an "animal" urge that must be satisfied once in a while, but she's not likely to risk her heart again.

Some days I understand the way she feels, and wonder if that is what is in store for me. Other days I long for attachment, for the bond I see between couples holding hands as they walk down the street or nestling against each other in restaurant banquettes. As a writer, I crave solitude

Evelyn Lau

and cling to my earned independence. I have always been fascinated by marriage, by what binds people together, but cannot seem to imagine it for myself. For a long time I wanted to believe that there was only one person in the world for me, or for that matter for anyone—that love was singular and unmistakeable and once-in-a-lifetime. I didn't understand how a feeling as powerful as love could change to hatred or indifference. I remember reading about a prominent businessman who, during his rancorous divorce, yelled into his wife's answering machine, "I promise God I will destroy you!" How do you go from wanting with everything in your heart to protect the person you have chosen, to that?

I want to trust in the permanence of love, to believe that desire can last. But the reality is that I seem incapable of forming a relationship based on mutuality. I look at my friends in their thirties, married to people their own age, starting a life together with a house and a mortgage and two jobs and thoughts of children. I see how they truly have a partnership, but that is the last thing I want for myself. The thought of sharing my life as an equal with another person almost repulses me. It doesn't coincide with my fantasy of finding a father figure, something that goes right through all the structures of my being.

So, at twenty-seven, I find myself back in my psychiatrist's office. He is the safest person I know. He looked after me during my adolescence; this past year, as an adult, I started seeing him again. In some ways I never left; he has always inhabited me, my deepest thoughts, my dreams. I know a little more about him now than I did before, yet the distance is still there, the stern gulf between doctor and patient. But we sometimes banter and laugh, and I suppose someone listening to us would think we sound like two people who have known each other for a long time, which we have. I occasionally desire him, in a wistful sort of way. He is roundish, with a soft, genial face. I often arrive early for our sessions, for the tense pleasure of waiting for him at the top of the staircase like I used to wait for my father to come home from work, clamouring to be the first to greet him, the smell and the scratch of his tweed jacket against my face. Then at the bottom of the stairs I see the doctor's thick, cherubic body as he enters the building, and I am flooded with the same relief—he has not come to harm, he has not forgotten me. I see the preoccupied look on his face, his smile when I call down to him. The keys jangle in his hand as he pounds up the stairs, unlocks the door, lets me in.

There are days I long to climb into his lap, curl up there like a child or a kitten, and indeed when I can't sleep I sometimes picture myself that way, as small as a doll in his lap. But what makes this desire possible is the necessary distance between us. I know I will never sit in his lap, that he will never threaten or destroy me by reaching out for me. Without the mercurial tides of sexual involvement, desire can sometimes be as uncomplicated as this—wanting to feel safe, held in another's gaze and attention, in that constant and unchanging light.

CHANGING
INTO FIRE

Lorna Crozier

CHANGING

INTO FIRE

c r o q i e r

I N A S M A L L R O O M in a monastery in Saskatchewan
I am writing desire. You, my companion of twenty
years, seem so far away, farther than the rolling miles
and the mountains that rise between my room and our
house on the Coast. My time alone here is a gift, each day
wrapped in tissue as if the dates were etched on a calendar
made of glass. I have two weeks—fourteen days—to write
and read, to walk and dream this snowy landscape, to miss

you in the luxurious way old lovers know when their separation is a choice. Desire is both here and there, both inside and outside my body. Nothing is more alive to the present—the tastes and smells—yet desire has a past, chapters in a life, a ghostly history. When I touch myself, it is memory I arouse, my body dancing the oldest dance on the tip of a finger. Where did it begin for me? How did I learn to love myself and then love you? I am sending these words across the snow and mid-February cold. I can see you sitting in the blue chair, opening my letters with your comely hands, one cat in your lap. On the windowsill the other cat cleans his whiskers and watches the rain that falls between us.

The faucet between the taps in the old claw-footed bathtub swelled into a bulb in the middle, then straightened out again. If I sat close to the front of the tub, knees bent, I could see a naked miniature of my ten-year-old self reflected in the faucet's shiny globe. When I turned the white enamel handles of the taps, warm water rushed between my legs, and I felt something I'd never felt before, a stirring in my flesh. My small double was the only other

Lorna Crozier

one who knew. There's an innocence here that wasn't to last, an unsullied moment before the world interfered. At ten, I was completely aware of my body, yet at the same time outside it, observing, creating from my naked self my own object of desire.

Do you see this girl? Do you feel the heat as steam rises above the tub and mists the window? She is the one who is always there. In my mind's eye she raises water in her hands to her soon-to-be breasts and lets the warmth rain over them. Like shallow pools the mirrors in the room hold the water's glisten and the girl, opening. In a poem you've written *mirrors are windows with a memory*. How far back they go depends upon how much we can bear to see. The girl watches herself watching, and then she watches you, her image in your eyes. You sit on the edge of the tub and lift the washcloth that gleams with the last of light rinsed from her limbs and hold it out for me.

There is so much silence surrounding desire, yet the mouth is the first part of the body to act on what it wants—that cry in the birth room, wide open, then the sucking and the thin rivulet of milk. When the mouth is dumb it is most smooth and eloquent, moving across another, lip-reading. What mother tongue for this? The erotics of not speaking. A pout at the bottom of the letter, a lipstick kiss mouthing a word.

My childhood friend and I learned to kiss in her basement room, the sound of her mother's footsteps above our heads. We started with smacking our lips on our arms, loving the rudeness of that sound, the crazy laughter. My arms were covered with blonde fuzz, and I was proud of them. I wanted them to be as strong and hairy as my father's. I loved the slick trail my tongue left above my wrist as if a snail had slid there; I loved the whiff of brown, sun-soaked skin. I still raise my forearm to my nose in summer and inhale deeply. A pleasure that remains exquisite and taboo. "What are you doing?" you ask, and I don't tell you.

Once her mother called from the top of the stairs, "What's going on down there?" and we leapt apart like startled deer. By then, we had moved beyond mere kissing. "Telling stories" was what we called it, and narratives were essential to our pleasure, our make-believe inspiring bravery, the discovery of the musky secrets of our flesh. Did

Lorna Crozier

our mothers say, "Don't touch yourself?" I can't remember but it seems likely. Otherwise, why the guilt, the silence?

We took turns, she being the man and me the woman, and then we reversed the roles. For a time the woman was Debbie Reynolds, then Sandra Dee, and finally Carroll Baker in her baby doll pajamas. The man was always Randolph Scott, a cowboy dangerous and gruff, not like Roy or Audie, though we liked Audie's shortness and his cute smile. Randolph, we thought, could make a woman do anything and she wouldn't feel bad about it. We kissed each other in my friend's basement room; we touched, our fingers smelling of that special smell, snowdrifts covering the window, her mother making supper, the phone ringing above us, my mother on the other end calling me home.

In its speaking, what the poem craves is silence. We hear it in the haiku masters, each character clean and sharply drawn, yet in between hoarfrost grows, fragile enough to break with the lightest touch. When I stand outside in the prairie sun and cold, dozens of crystals sift from a pine bough and settle on my hair and shoulders. Breaking the stasis with its small weight, a red-capped finch has landed above my head, the hoarfrost falling. Otherwise, before the bird begins to sing, I wouldn't know it was there.

My friend and I always sang on our way home from school. Her voice was so lovely I convinced myself it was mine. I broke into song with everything I had until a teacher put me in the back with the tone-deaf boys told to mouth the words. Forty years later, I rarely see my friend, but when I do we don't talk about those times; we don't sing. In the polite European way, to avoid the smudge of lipstick, our mouths glance lightly off each other's cheeks and kiss the air. It's as if the snow that fell on everything in our childhood has erased the memory of our clandestine time together. Until this moment, you're the only one I've told. *I love the way you kiss*, you say. It must be all that practice. During the long winters, we tell each other stories in our bed. I am the woman; you, the man, though sometimes we switch places, you on your back with your legs in the air. You do what I tell you and you don't feel bad. I have a dangerous edge.

At the monastery, I'm staying in the building where the nuns once lived. Forty years they cooked and cleaned for

Lorna Crozier

the monks until there were too few to do the work; the remaining elderly sisters moved into a retirement home in town. The mattresses on the narrow beds have never been replaced. Mine is soft and lumpy. It's hard not to think of the nun who once slept here, the temptations of the flesh. What would she have called her sin or the soft nub her fingers touched when they slipped from her rosary, full of grace?

"Down there" was what my mother called it. The words made me tingle with excitement and fear. "Down there" also meant the cellar with its earthen walls and floors, its shelves of canning, the bins of softening potatoes scabbed with mud, the smell of damp and darkness. Something was always just behind me as I ran up the wooden stairs, a sealer in my hand, the nape of my neck prickling. Down there was dangerous. Down there was where your hand shouldn't wander, and later, where a boy shouldn't touch you. A no man's land, my mother hoped, down there.

The object of a date was not the boy himself. The fun and sexual buzz were most delicious in the hour or so of getting ready—the pink of the powder puff dusting my skin, the satiny cold cream rubbed lovingly on each toe and up my calves to the top of my thighs, the backcombing, the hairspray, the quick dab of Evening of Paris in the hollow of my neck, the tiny samples of lipstick tubes from Avon lined up on the dresser, their names full of promise: Ravishing Red, Candy Kiss, Peach Delight. As I struggled with the zipper in the back of my dress, I whispered, "Darling, can you help me do this up?" I pouted my lips and gauged the effect of a bra strap slipping down my shoulder. Desire was a smell in the air, a sound, the swish of nylons as I walked from dresser to closet to mirror, then swept out of my parents' house into the night.

Unfortunately the night wasn't Evening in Paris but Evening in Swift Current, and the boy waiting at the door was not the debonair figure who had helped me with my dress. Later, in his dad's car, he was overly insistent and awkward, hasty and sometimes sloppily sentimental. Surely it wasn't his eyes—or hands—I had preened for. No: what saved the evening were the other boys, boys whose gaze I'd catch at the dance or the movie, boys I knew only distantly or not at all. Among them there must be one who was waiting just for me. Everything hung on that possibil-

Lorna Crozier

ity. The conviction that I would meet him fanned the sparks, the electric craving for the stranger who would change my life forever.

In this Saskatchewan winter I'm rediscovering snow. How to tell you of its lusciousness! I get down on my hands and knees and lick it, leaving the track of my tongue beside the small exquisite paw prints of a mouse. I listen to snow's silky slide from hood to boots; I stand under a streetlight and watch the tiniest stars lift and fall in the wind. I, too, float above the ground, drifting in some middle halfway place, part earth, part sky, my mouth remembering how fire can live inside such cold.

In the Coldstream mill, you pulled lumber on the green chain eight hours a day. Three kids and a wife. Still in high school, I wouldn't have known what that meant. Every Saturday night, you'd put the kids to bed in the trailer, go to the bar with the childhood sweetheart you'd married in grade twelve, order a hamburger and a beer and pretend you were happy. You didn't know yet that she was sleeping with your friend.

Saturday nights I went to bed guilty because some boy had touched my breasts and I had liked it. I didn't tell anyone about either the pleasure or the frustration of those evenings: an Everly Brothers' song on the car radio; a mouth here; a hand there; buttons, clasps and zippers undoing, unhooking, sliding down—*whoa!* Everything would stop as I struggled with my fear of the consequences, the boy sometimes angry, both of us unsatisfied, the lust fizzing out. It would be twelve years before you and I would meet each other, then another two before you'd drive from Golden to Fort Qu'Appelle to find me, leaving another wife and different kids behind. Before all that, one night as you counted out your change in the Coldstream bar, I stood in front of the mirror, making my mouth as red as it could be, using up all the colour in the Avon tube as if I could make the brightness last, as if it could travel to where you were, lovely stranger, lighting a cigarette and sending its glow into the dark.

Desire is a restless ghost. It taps on our windows with the small knuckles of the rain, keeps us awake all hours of the night, arriving in shapes we least expect the way a poem comes sometimes out of longing. Tonight in my small

Lorna Crozier

room I crave to see my father's hands. How I loved to look at them, lean, work-worn, large-jointed, the lines in his palms stained with grease and machine oil. They were so graceful. They played the light around my mother's body with the thin bow of a violin at the schoolhouse dances in Success. I slept with the other kids on a pile of coats in the cloakroom after the communal supper. Then the dancing, the talk and the coaxing towards the end of evening until my father got up to play. I never heard him, or at least not that I can recall. When I was four, he sold his violin to buy a combination record player and radio. It sat in the living room, huge and dark, not quite fitting against the wall. Before I learned to be embarrassed by what my parents loved, I sat beside them on the couch and listened to Wilf Carter, the Sons of the Pioneers, Hank Williams and Hank Snow, the Chuckwagon Gang, and the singing movie cowboys: *Rock me to sleep in my saddle. I shall miss your bright eyes and sweet smile. Till we meet again.*

You say you noticed how I looked at your hands the first day we met. Every opportunity, you'd lay them on the table. Before my father got sick, you and he could have matched palms, your fingers fitting perfectly on top of his. On a piece of paper the outline would have looked the same. You'd come to Regina as a poet, but that year you'd been building houses to make a living, staying up all night with the blueprints so the owner, who worked alongside you, wouldn't know you'd never done this before. You'd blackened the nail of your thumb and scraped three knuckles raw. Years later you took me to see the house and it was standing solid on a rock, dormer windows gazing at the sea in Half Moon Bay.

Did I know it was my father's hands I was seeing, their shadow behind yours? The thickness and beauty hard work brings to the sinews and muscles around the finger bones, as if all the things they'd held had left behind a sheen. I would have given anything for you to touch me. For you to stroke soft music, your work-worn fingers moving through my hair.

Every bone in the body has a name. Occipital, femur, cranium, ulna and clavicle, where my father rested his violin. Why are there so few names for other things that matter—loss and longing, all the variations of woe? Here wind presses the shape of its ribs into the snowdrifts. I count

Lorna Crozier

them to see if the lower one is missing, to see if wind, solitary in this vast space, carves its lover over and over from loneliness, thin and white.

You've broken almost every one of your bones. When you list them it's an anatomy of pain and mending. The last break was your ankle; your brother called me in Saskatoon to tell me you'd jumped off a cliff. Fifty years old and you'd leapt into an Okanagan river because you'd seen what fun the kids were having flying through the air. On the hospital phone just before your surgery, you didn't say you shouldn't have done it. Instead you told me you'd misjudged the distance: one foot hit the clay shore inches from the water. *I should have jumped farther, Babe,* you said.

At home in a cast from groin to ankle, you leaned naked, one arm on each counter in the corner of the kitchen. You were so weak and pale. I slid a soapy cloth down your chest and belly, held your penis in my hand like a fallen fledgling, pushed back the hood of skin and rubbed gently, then ran the washcloth down your bare leg to your foot. On the leg with the cast, I could wash only your toes. Your body so bright, I can't tell you what I felt—not desire but something like it flew up from my pelvis, fluttered in my rib cage and my throat. How I longed to touch and touch and not let go.

Desire should be a longer word, multisyllabic. There's such a distance in it, a wish for the absent to be present. A thousand miles away, you tell me it has rained and rained, our basement flooding. I reply with wind and snow. You're thawing a chicken breast for supper. You'll fry it with red peppers, ginger and some oyster mushrooms you found on sale. I'm thinking of goldeye in a white wine sauce. All this chat about the weather and our evening meals! We could be brother and sister, mother and son. Is this all there is to talk about after twenty years? Why are we settling for so little?

I hang up the phone and look through the book I've kept this week on my bedside table. It's a collection of ancient stories from the desert fathers who sought wisdom in solitude. I find the parable I'm seeking: One of the fathers feels he's missing something in his daily tasks. He consults his elder. "According as I am able," he says, "I keep my little rule, my little fast, my prayer and meditation. I strive to cleanse my heart of thoughts. What more should I do?" The elder rises up and stretches his hands to heaven, his fingers ten lamps flaring. *Why not be totally changed into fire?* When you see me next, you may not recognize my body, but you'll know the heat I bring you, its slow lick and sizzle.

Last summer in the garden you palmed the sun simmering beneath the skin of our first ripe tomato. What to do with a man who ate it whole, putting half inside his mouth and biting down? Seeds, pulp and juice ran through your fingers and down your shirt. *Pomodoro. Love apple.* The Chinese thought it poisonous. There's a bit of the devil in you, taking a risk, denying the thin slice with salt and basil. This was going to be our supper, you glutton, with bacon and mayonnaise on pieces of bread. Your second bite—the air burned up; the leaves on our tomato plant and I unbuttoned. What was green reddened, what was sour sweetened, what was fruit and flesh burst into flames between your teeth.

You and I saw each other clearly, for the first time, over a line of poetry. Do you remember? It was after the workshop where we met, after supper and the reading you gave in the gallery in Regina. In my high, Cuban-heeled boots, I was tall and dancing on your words. At a party twenty people gathered to listen to a radio broadcast of Saskatchewan poetry. You sprawled on the couch, a whiskey in your hand, a young woman sitting on the floor beside you. I knew you'd leave together. Trying not to look at you, I sat across the room in a straight-backed kitchen chair. Your hand rested on her shoulder; her eyes closed like a cream-fed cat's as she slumped against your shins. I wanted to drag her away, I wanted to say something brilliant and necessary to show you what you were missing.

On the radio, another poet described himself watching a woman planting seeds. *If I kept a journal*, he read, *I'd say: Today she was beautiful.* I lifted my head. You did too, and we stared at one another. *And if I kept a diary, I'd say: Today I was beautiful.* We saw each other, keenly, as a poem sees what it is praising, as a woman sees a man and a man sees a woman. At that moment both of them know this is the person they will one day love.

The lubricious syllables of flowers said out loud in February: *camellia, magnolia, foxglove.* In my palm for the chickadees and nuthatches I offer black seeds from the monk's dried

Lorna Crozier

sunflowers that stared so brazenly in the summer garden, their huge heads nodding. *No* is not a word in their vocabulary, round-faced *yes* of blossoms, completely open whether or not the seeds have time to ripen. This is desire's flower, not oleander or the rose. A bride should carry them to her groom, their thick stalks bristly as they're passed from hand to hand. In the morning the seed heads must be moved from the bridal chamber to somewhere in the winter garden where birds will gather, stirring new affection for the sun.

Throughout my marriage I was waiting for you, though I didn't know it. At twenty, I thought I'd married for love, but I'd chosen a man I could leave when I was ready. He was a safe place, a sanctuary I returned to after nights of infidelity. For eight years I waited for him to tell me to go. How selfish I was, how cowardly! Only months after we split up, he wed again, and soon he had a child, a daughter tall and blonde. Our mutual friends tell me he's devoted. The pleasure she gives him is one of my blessings, one of the ways I can forgive myself though she and I will never meet.

You and I met for the second time at a writers' conference in Saskatoon. Two years had passed since I'd first seen you. You seemed so arrogant, so sure of yourself. Bold and sassy, I disagreed with everything you said until you pulled me from the table in the bar into the hall. You put your arms around me and we kissed—then, I didn't disagree. In your hotel room, missing the case for my contact lenses, I stuck them on a cup and with a ballpoint pen wrote "r" above one and "l" above the other, the nib sinking in the styrofoam. By morning they had shrivelled. I was blind for you; I was lost. When I walked you to the gate at the airport, I was wearing turquoise sandals. "How beautiful your toes," you said, "in turquoise shoes."

The photograph I've placed by my narrow nun's bed was taken last summer in Japan, a place I've never been. On the stepping stones that cross a pond in the famous garden in Kyoto, you kneel, straw hat in one hand, the other reaching over the water. A golden koi lifts to your pointing finger. That's the way I rose when you first touched me, my whole body gleaming.

So much between lovers is invisible. I don't see any deer when I go for my walks around the abbey grounds, but their hoofprints criss-cross the roads and field. Numerous as sparrows, in early morning they must tread their paths while I sleep. What you see when you look closely is their longing—their tracks shaped like the hinged V of maple seeds, as if with every step there's a planting, small delicate movements towards spring.

When I come back inside, I find an envelope someone has slid beneath my door. A letter from you! Halfway through, there's a break when you list what you'll to do to me when I get home—*Christ!* you write and disappear off the page. Then you're back again, saying the right hand moves the pen more smoothly than the left. This is where I want to be, in that pause with you, that lacuna. Even the cats are missing me, you write. In our bed the female curled next to your head and purred as you held yourself, her black paw on your ear.

Two months after that night in Saskatoon, I said good-bye to my husband and drove to teach a summer workshop in the Qu'Appelle Valley. "See you in two weeks," I said to him. I had every intention of going back. Later, I would discover you pulled out of Golden that same day, heading east in an old white Ford. You'd told me on the phone you were coming to get me. I wasn't sure you meant it, and I didn't know what I'd do if you arrived. You were so bad you were good for me; I knew that if I hurt you, you could hurt me back.

In the valley by the lake, I sensed something different against my skin, as if the force of your car speeding through the wind stirred the air around me. I'd never wanted anyone so much. That summer Bonnie Tyler's "It's a Heartache" blared from every radio. I imagined you on the road inside the song, July heat bouncing off the pavement and roaring in the windows, your black T-shirt wet with sweat. The button on your jeans could burn a finger.

Five screws joined the pieces of your ankle bone together. A few months after the cast came off, one worked itself out, puncturing your skin. A doctor removed it with a small screwdriver and sewed three stitches. We put the screw in a bowl where we save stones, sea glass and bits of tile from places like Palenque and the Baths of Caracalla, ruins we've visited together, the little that's survived crumbling at a footfall, the touch of a breath, the blue beat of a butterfly's wings. In such places we grow old, years accumulating on our skin their fine grey dust. Two inches of stainless steel that once lived in your body glint among these fragments. Some nights I hold that shining metal tight inside my fist to keep from crying out.

❖

The last and first names of things: the woman I become when we lie together. The self-love of early childhood, small replica in the bathtub's silver faucet, a girl kissing her own arm, tongue touching the tongue of her friend, their sweet forbidden music; Saturday night cologne in the hollow of my throat, alive in my skin, then and now pleasuring me and pleasuring you, the quiet healing of your bones, their lexicon of mending—*today I am beautiful*—hoarfrost on the strings of a violin. Everything coming together without shame. Your hands hold so much, what the eye can bear to see. The gleam of fish rising in a pond, first snow falling on a page. Desire, I will look for you at the gate to our garden, my hair on fire.

SILENCE AND EXCEPTION

Bonnie Burnard

SILENCE

AND EXCEPTION

burnard

THE IDEA OF DISCUSSING desire does not entice me much. Perhaps this is because the thing I value most about intimacy, and intimacy is the place where desire thrives, is that it is *intimate*. It is exclusive. It seems to me that desire is one of those human undertakings, like childbirth, like war, like cancer or any other serious illness, that simply cannot be comprehended by someone who is not directly engaged. Undertakings. Engaged. You see my difficulty.

1.

Desire *has* been on my mind these past few months. Although almost all of the characters in my novel *A Good House* indulge in sexual activity, and although this activity is extremely varied, from honest to cold-blooded, from perfunctory to robust to languid, I have discovered that I cannot know, cannot truly comprehend their desires from the inside of their bodies. And, because after four years of involvement many of these characters have become good friends of mine, I find myself reluctant to intrude. I have tried to comprehend every other aspect of my characters from the inside. I have caused them to expose some intensely private matters, because that's what fiction writers do. So what's the difference, I wonder?

The women I know in my real life, my actual friends, do talk, almost always honestly and without much prompting, about many, many things. Around and between modest news of achievement and the eager communication of occasional fits of happiness, they don't hesitate to confess astonishing mistakes, moral shortcomings and lifelong regrets. But the women I have known longest and best, articulate, forthright women, do not describe their desire. It is a given

Bonnie Burnard

that they feel or have felt desire and expect to feel it again, but they don't speak it, they don't put it into words.

And the men in my real life? Have they spoken desire? Yes, some of them have, but always with an understanding that their words would not be recounted out in the world, examined after the act in the unsympathetic light of day, used for other purposes. And anyway, given that the hard evidence of desire and its endlessly particular delivery are so very appealing, who wants to be distracted by mere words?

Perhaps I believe, perhaps I have always believed that talk kills desire, that these two wondrous functions simply should not, cannot, coexist. This separation might be a physiological fact, one of the body's most trustworthy regulating mechanisms, like swallowing and breathing, with that little miracle of design, the epiglottis, flopping around in our throats ensuring that our bodies do just the one thing at a time, guarding against the discomfort of air in our guts, the danger of chunks of undigested food in our lungs.

There are sounds that echo desire. Mama Cass singing "Dream a Little Dream of Me" and Rufus Wainwright's take on "Young Love" almost do it for me. There have been others. But these are more than aching words put to catchy tunes. This is singing; it is need delivered by a living, breathing cadence, the aching of one warm heart made real by raw inflection.

And there are images that almost suffice. For me it's usually a depiction of deep water and boats and a large-boned figure, a lone man occupied with work, or concentrating. A storm (thunder, not ice) can come very close, perhaps because thunder and lightning make their own rules, come when they will, and change the air, the entire air.

But when desire is examined too aggressively, it must give itself over to words. It must become *idea*. It has to make the leap to a different nervous system, the one that talks and argues and stores and processes all other ideas, and rarely leaves you with a satisfied smile on your face. When we talk desire, aren't we coaxing, badgering, trying to take control? I have never wanted control.

To bring desire to life in my characters, I would have to assign to them variations on my own experience, because this is all I truly know. Such an approach strikes me as far too limiting, and therefore, in some important way, invalid. I have examined desire very closely in short fiction, but not often. My story "Crush" describes a girl who courageously

B o n n i e   B u r n a r d

exposes her breasts to a bread man in a small-town kitchen. In spite of the strength of her nervy lust and the confused response of his erection, I suspect that this study of young risk was simply a way to condone or accept or forgive my own puzzling behaviour when I was an inept beginner who could see nothing of interest in innocence. And, perhaps, by proxy, to offer the possibility of a similar resolution in someone who might read the story.

I quite fearlessly do give my fictional characters joy and greed and grief and wisdom and foolishness and, occasionally, redemption, all of which are surely as internal as desire. But compared to desire, these states, these shades of the human condition, are easy to replicate, a relative piece of literary cake. Perhaps this is because each of them carries with it a particular language, a history as long as the literature associated with its existence, words capable of conveying true, or nearly true, meaning. Certainly desire carries its own language, perhaps the fullest possible range of language, from "How do I love thee?" to some variation on "I Wanna Hump Your Bitch Body Now," but it seems to me that when we try to speak our desire, words can only fail us, mightily. And that this failure is not a bad thing.

2.

If it is difficult to imagine parents in the act of love, it is impossible to imagine the force that brought them together. Their longing came to life in a realm beyond our own existence; a good part of it was probably at its peak in the time before we were conceived. Children witness and are the inevitable victims or beneficiaries of their parents' anger and ambition and regrets and pride and achievements, but not of their desire. Desire has nothing to say across the divide that separates one generation from another. It is best born new, each time, in each new body.

I have never talked about desire with my daughters or my son. How would I dare? And why? To ease their inevitable confusion? To heighten their anticipation? To stop hurt before it starts? I could try, I suppose, in the belief that knowledge sometimes intensifies experience or precludes foolishness, or at least the fullest repercussions of foolishness. I have worked hard to praise my children and to free them and protect them from everything else under the sun. They know their strengths, at least in some small part, because I have named them. They have been thoroughly immunized against disease. Their teeth are close to perfect. I have warned them about the high cost of apathy and inattention and about the misery that can result when trust is offered to a dangerous, careless friend. I have made a sixteen-year-old daughter slam on the brakes in an icy, empty parking lot so she could gain a visceral understanding of loss of control, and how it might be regained. But that was only ice.

Kids are smart, as were most of us, I suspect. They get busy creating the privacy they need almost immediately after they recognize their need for it. They wisely and effectively throw up the barriers of evasion and silence. Long before they own their independence, they understand their entitlement to private thoughts. And what are those private thoughts about? They are probably not about rivalry among friends, or insecurity with appearance, or the blunt cruelty of a teacher, or the coveting of a jacket exactly like that one *please*, because these are the things you do hear about, either daily or eventually. These are the thoughts that find articulation, that demand the response of either agreement or door-slamming debate. I would bet quite a bit of money that their most private thoughts are quietly biding their time, confidently waiting for that other kind of expression, hoping for its quick arrival and trusting its power before they are able to truly comprehend it. Surely this first insistence on boundaries is essential to the development of a desiring self.

I do sometimes rage against the culture that invades (shapes?) my kids' most intimate thoughts. I mourn the loss of their truest privacy, the chance for a slow, unique, unseen accumulation of image and nuance and gaze and hope and courage. Some of us who came through the heat of adolescence in the fifties have complained that we were cruelly ill-informed, that silence was a bad teacher, that learning it all on our own made us clumsy, or hesitant, or just stupid. But the time of silence is long gone. Its place has been taken by three lesser approaches: the clinical explanation (which is fair enough, I suppose, if only it could be done without butchering the mystery); the wonder of marketing (which teaches that a desirable body can get you great stuff, that stuff is way better than love, that stuff is in fact what desire really wants); and the often astonishingly grotesque representation of grown-up, mature desire.

Last week I rented one of Woody Allen's recent films. I must have been curious to see if Allen's deterioration

Bonnie   Burnard

was continuing apace because it's been some time since his vision had anything new to say to me. A few years ago I read that he suffers terribly from styes, infections of the eyelid. I just happen to have a cure for styes (a gold ring, rubbed lightly), and I thought about sending it along to him, probably because doing so would make a good story. But then I thought, he has so fouled longing, let the creep suffer.

I watched part of the film and then my daughter watched it later, on her own, as a respite from the writing of an essay. Seeing her stretched out on the sofa, hearing Woody and company reduce the pleasure, the complexity of desire to fucking this and fucking that, to mere and pathetic ego, I thought, How godawful for her, to see this now, just when her own tentative desire should be coming into its fullest, ground-shifting strength.

But if I had broached this with my daughter, if I had stepped across the divide, I know she would have told me, as she has before, casually, "This is nothing." And she would have been right.

When I calculate the words and images that my kids have been offered by their culture, Allen's slimy, self-loathing, self-loving study of desire *is* nothing. How odd it must be, and how very new, for young women to watch a thousand times over as the self they want so much to become (smart, pretty, sexy) is not just raped and murdered but raped dead, eviscerated, decapitated, with the camera loving it, the camera moving in as close as a lover to watch.

After kids pass a certain age, censure is useless, and it's likely that the normal disclaimer, "It's only mindless Hollywood junk," does not offer much solace against the clear and continuous evidence that the death of a sexy young woman can evoke not gut-wrenching fear or horror or grief but that far better thing, the shared public coming: excitement. For a long time we have agreed to watch good men murdered for our entertainment, but when men are murdered the camera cannot take the time to linger lovingly or long on the corpse because almost immediately it must swing away to follow the action, the revenge, the retribution. For the most part boys still have the comfort of imagining that if they were harmed, some bigger, better, stronger guy would soon ride up on a horse or in a tank or a Porsche to make it right, cost be damned, danger be damned. With few exceptions, the camera has never got off on the death of men.

Bonnie   Burnard

And then there's the stench of advertising, the crass inundation of things sexual that surrounds the make-believe. The commercials that bring us the promises of delivery, the admonitions to chew this gum or buy these yellow high-heeled sandals or smell like this or put this wondrous gunk in our hair, do not seem to have freed any of the spirits I know, not noticeably. The guarantee that if they will only consume they will cause or feel arousal does not seem to have released the young from doubt or fear or confusion. They do not seem to be taking strength from these cultural imperatives, this pseudo-sophistication, this pond scum of the heart. Although they have been exposed to truckloads of sexual imagery, the young people I see and listen to seem to me still only young, and private, and funny, and sometimes lonely, and sometimes courageous. They are the most beautiful creatures on earth, surely as pristine as angels in their raunchy, secret longing (as was I) and just as surely bewildered by the leering, lucrative prurience that wraps itself around and around desire. And, oh, I want to tell them, it's not like that. It's nothing like that.

3.

When I do hear talk of desire, most often between women about men, it almost always arises obliquely, and often with soft laughter folded in, for protection. Or it can take the form of one of those nearly inaudible chortles of recognition that says, Yes, I know. The women I count as my friends take this etiquette, this not really telling, very seriously. The silence announces a profound loyalty to the man in question, who could be a husband or a long-past or just-discovered lover, and it most certainly represents an unspoken love for the moment of intimacy. Nice girls don't tell? Maybe. But quite a few bad girls don't tell either. Trust me on this.

Still, there is some fun to be had, obliquely. I indulge as often as any woman, and I know precisely where and when I first learned how to do it. I was fifteen and leaving a dance with three or four girlfriends, all of whom were slightly older, maybe seventeen. The town was close to a peacetime army camp, so the dance floor was always filled with young soldiers in training. Walking to the car, regrouping, my friends talked back and forth about the night they'd had, how that one guy was so funny, that other one so quiet, that other one so handsome, *such a hunk*. I had spent the last hour

B o n n i e   B u r n a r d

of the dance in the capable arms of a very tall, very good-looking young man (oh my yes, and isn't it a fine thing, the way that kind of memory sticks, the way one specific, hour-long moment of desire can be so entirely, so precisely recalled) and when my friends asked if I'd had a good time, I said, yes, I had, but I was pretty sure I was going to have bruises all over my stomach in the morning. This was long before any of us could imagine ourselves or any other woman actually bruised by a man.

I had not yet seen or reached to hold a penis. Nor was I certain before speaking that the mention of a bruised stomach would bring laughter, but I'd suspected it might and I was correct. Raucous laughter. What a perfect evening: held close for an entire hour, wrapped in the music I loved (forgotten now), walking confidently across a parking lot protected by the ease of friendship, and then that first burst of grown-up, female, *knowing* laughter.

I had not a drop of sympathy for my young soldier. Although that obvious rubbing, which should have been no more shocking than the easily given pressure of my breast against his ribs (I have always thought of my right breast as my dancing breast), was not a particularly refined seduction, it was almost certainly intended to be a shared event. But the hour of dancing was not about him, it was about me. It was my hour of discovery. It could be said that I was a cruel and selfish young woman, although I had accepted without question the party line, delivered in a brief, shy lecture by the home economics teacher in a few illicit moments between the slipstitch and the lifelong merits of a good white sauce, that it was harder for guys, that we should understand that it was harder for guys, and watch ourselves. Did my soldier laugh too, riding back out to the army camp with his buddies? Or were his fists clenched, was he annoyed, ticked off that once again a warm body had been offered and then coldly removed? I had known precisely what it was that rested (wrong word, of course) against me, and he would have known that I knew. Was he smart enough, kind enough to guess that I was only young, and learning? Perhaps girls have too little expectation of sexual rejection; it was certainly not one of the things we feared that summer, or any other. Many of us have become familiar with other kinds of denial, and sometimes in spades. But not that kind. Rarely that kind.

Within a few years my evenings ended somewhere else

and very differently. For a time there wasn't much raucous female laughter because, for a time, the friendship of women receded, pulling back quite naturally and amicably, returning later with the comfort of other kinds of knowing, when the babies started to arrive, when a career began to develop.

This was the period in my life when desire played itself out most fiercely, when desire was least like idea, most like itself. And the time of *absolute* loyalty. When I look at some of the words that align themselves with loyalty (firmness, duty, perseverance, fidelity), they seem completely appropriate. To the man and to the moment.

I have loved and still love equally the necessary, nurturing silence of intimacy and after-the-fact reassurance from others of my kind, from women, that my desire is a thing known to them, that it is safe and funny and heart-wrenching and good, and true for us all. Necessary and nurturing to me at least. Reassuring to me.

If I were to try to speak desire here, this one time, this only time, I might use the words *mine* and *yours* and then, to join these two, I might choose the word *gift*. But even this combination of words is paltry. It speaks of longing as ash speaks of fire, as bones describe flesh. It says nothing.

PHOTO
PARENTHESES

Shani Mootoo

PHOTO

PARENTHESES

m o o t o o

THERE IS A PHOTOGRAPH of me taken when I was not yet five years old. One of the faculties I am simultaneously blessed and cursed with is a memory as long as time, and I remember well the day I posed for this photo. I was in the care of my maternal grandparents in Trinidad then; my parents were living in Ireland so that my father could study medicine. As the picture was to be sent to them, my grandmother insisted that

I wear a dress, a frilly thing with a crinoline. I was equally determined to wear a short-pant sailor suit: navy-blue shorts, navy-blue top with a white bib edged with two rows of red piping, and blue cloth-topped shoes. I can still recall Ma's voice, high-pitched and hoarse with frustration as she pleaded with me.

In the photo I stand atop a concrete garden stool in a fenced-in corner of my grandparents' garden. I am dressed in the sailor suit. My skin is pale, my body plump with the love and tenderness of overindulgent adults. My chubby hands hang clasped in shyness in front of me. My long hair, the pride of my grandparents, is pulled back in a ponytail. A casual observer would have noticed the smile and sturdy posture of a well-loved, good-natured girl child.

But under the skin there was the odd sensation that I did not fit in my body well. That my body was not my own. That while I was supposed to look and dress and "behave" like a girl, I had doubts that I was. For many years to come I was convinced it would one day be revealed, to everyone's surprise but mine, that I was a boy after all. At the time of the picture-taking session I had not yet told my grandmother that one of Pa's card-playing pals was touch-

S h a n i   M o o t o o

ing me in ways that made me frightened. Consequently, she had not yet had the opportunity to tell me, as she eventually did, that I should never say such words again.

My first urgent yearning: to break out of the body in which a more real, more substantial me was trapped.

When I was barely six years old my parents returned to live in Trinidad. They enrolled me in an all-girl primary school run by nuns. The Christmas I was seven, my school and the exclusively female secondary school also attached to the convent joined forces to put on the play *Babes in Toyland*. The play's main character, a young man named Alan, owns a little army of toy soldiers who have a propensity for bursting into song. The story is about Alan's quest for the hand of the woman he loves. I was intrigued and tickled that the part of Alan was being played by Maria, a secondary-school prefect. I played the part of one of Alan's toy soldiers, and I revelled in the opportunity to dress like a boy, to march about in a way that would never have been permitted girls in those days. My tall, black, cylindrical soldier's hat of stiffened felt, with a front brim and a chin strap and a high gold feather, was my treasure. I never wanted to be without it, even after the play had run its course. I can still smell the glue that held it together.

It was a dream come true to be a boy, even just for a couple of hours every few days. I studied Maria's movements on stage, and during intermissions I watched her, in moustache and men's clothing, strutting around with an air of confidence and pride that none of the other actors seemed to have. The woman Alan loved was played by a school prefect named Marilyn, the most beautiful, kindest girl I knew. Even during rehearsal breaks Marilyn hovered around Maria, who seemed possessive of her.

There is a scene in the play where Alan, usually surrounded by his toy soldiers, kisses his lover. During rehearsal of the kissing scene the convent folk made sure that there were no toy soldiers, the youngest members of the cast, on stage or even in the wings. On rehearsal days, we would perform our parts first and then be picked up by our parents while the rest of the rehearsal continued. One day some unsuspecting older student who had been given charge of me took me back into the theatre to await my pickup. I sat in the dark and watched the older students, and I got to see the kiss. I saw Alan kiss his girlfriend. I saw Maria kiss Marilyn; the blood in my body seemed to drain and rush back in all at once. My tummy quivered; my thighs tickled inexplicably. Never in my short life had I wished more to have been born a boy.

At the close of the school year my parents took my three siblings and me for a weekend's holiday on one of Trinidad's east-coast beaches. After we had settled into our hotel rooms, my sister and I went exploring. In the resort's restaurant, I was suddenly halted by what lay ahead, my breathing arrested. Facing away from us, but unmistakeable to me, was Marilyn. Once I spotted her, I was too shy to enter the room. She was sitting in a bathing suit at the bar, her long dark hair and perky posture compelling. There was a young man with her, his arm around her back. As my sister tried to drag me along, not knowing or caring what held my interest, I lingered for several seconds. I didn't watch Marilyn. I watched *him*, his shirtless muscled torso, his hard sinewy arm, his hand clutching her shoulder. I was mesmerized, dizzy and excited all at once. A waiter approached the couple, and from the way the man talked and gestured, telling the waiter what to do, I thought that the hotel must be his. Later that evening, while we ate supper at the restaurant, he came to the table to say hello to my parents and it was confirmed: the resort we stayed at was owned by his family.

For the next three days I was a live wire, sizzling, almost combustible with nervousness and confusion. During the day Marilyn and other young men and women hung out on a rooftop patio that overlooked the beach and the sea. They were all white-skinned. They wore sunglasses and had drinks in their hands; more drinks rested on the banister ledge and on the round outdoor plastic table. Though I was below them, down on the beach, in the periphery of my vision I was aware of Marilyn's every move. I had more energy than my little body could contain. Knowing that she was up there on the rooftop I would begin a ritual, running wildly down the damp sand close to the water's edge and then flinging myself on my knees, sliding along the coarseness that shimmered like ground glass until I came to a natural halt. Then I would get up and do it all over again. My knees at the end of the day were raw and bleeding, but I looked forward to more of the same. It was the most pleasurable bruising; it made my unspeakable, confusing attraction to that girl from *Babes in Toyland* almost tolerable. The following day, Marilyn again on the rooftop, I ran and dropped to my knees and slid, all with a perfection honed in the past night's dreams. Finally, to my utter shock, Marilyn called down to me. I ran to the edge of the roof's overhang and looked up at her, grinning. She smiled at me, and in a caring, almost teasing tone she said, "Shani, who are you falling for like that!" My face stung. I don't remember replying, though I do remember thinking, "For you, for you."

It didn't take me long to realize that the terse, whispered conversations and smouldering silences between my parents were spats. Eventually their altercations grew less discreet. When my mother found one of my father's shirts in the laundry, lipstick disingenuously displayed all along its collar, the tension in the air exploded and accusations ricocheted off the walls. My siblings and I learned that our father was intimately involved with another woman. To Mummy's mind Daddy was cheating on her, but it didn't take a leap of the imagination for us to feel that he was also cheating on us.

My mother's parents had long since died. There was no one else she felt she could trust with her confidences, so she called on me, the eldest child, for advice and support. Seeing her utter confusion and devastation, in my innocence I thought to myself, "She is so weak, so frail, so unappealing. No wonder . . ." But I didn't dare finish the sentence. Her life seemed suffocating. What I saw was a woman who stayed at home with her children, making sure the house was kept clean and tidy; who spent many evenings propped up in bed with a book in her lap, dozing like that as she waited. In contrast, to my mind my father was an amazingly charming man. I so admired him. I saw him with women and with men, saw how they hung on his every word, were eager to please him, to be seen saying hello to him; the men shaking his hand, the women greeting him with a kiss or a too-familiar hug. He was a politician who held various positions in government and in the opposition. He was a dynamic public figure, a man out and about in the world, day and night, having one adventure after another.

What I had always suspected was confirmed. To be a man was to do. To be a woman was to be done unto. My resolve renewed, I created for myself a mantra: Shed the body I was born into; never treat women in the ways I

S h a n i   M o o t o o

experienced myself and saw all around me; become a hero, a do-good cowboy so that I could save women, including my mother and my sisters, from harm.

My father was a veritable knight to all women, but as I watched him I began to detect slight differences in the kinds of charm he dispensed from one woman to the next. I took note of the characteristics of the ones he seemed disconcertingly captivated by and set out to lure. Long wavy dark-brown hair. Solidly, confidently squared to the ground, as if hips and pelvis were anchored there. Slim. Demure. Married. Pleasing, complimentary, deferential, jovial, always smiling. And White. Although my father was a professional man, being of Indian ancestry in a British colony, he and many others like him, no matter what they achieved, would never be the cream of society. A lowly businessman who was White had more clout than my highly educated, politically involved father.

Marilyn. She was White. She had wavy dark-brown hair, was built solidly, confidently squared to the ground, as if . . .

I was fifteen when a boy in my neighbourhood declared that he had fallen in love with me. After school, every time the phone rang, space would all but implode. Time would stop, so would my heart, and I would wait to be called, hoping it was him. If it wasn't, I would withdraw, sit on my bed with my homework idle in my lap. When he did ring, I would fly to the phone, barely able to breathe with delightful anticipation. We would speak for hours almost every evening for the short time that he was my "boyfriend." About books. About fresh-water fish-keeping and the scuba diving he often did with his father. About friends we had in common, the parties he was always inviting me to but I was never permitted to attend, the beaches he had explored by boat along the island's coastline. I practically lived for those calls, but they weren't as satisfying to him. Eventually he began to insist that we see each other, even suggested coming around to request permission from my father to take me out with a number of friends to the theatre. When I ended up alone with him at a friend's house he tried to kiss me, and I remember thinking, "No! Don't do that. You'll ruin it all. It's not what I want!" It took me a while to realize that what I actually wanted was not him, but to be like him. I had fallen in love, it is true, but only with the reflection of myself that I saw in him.

In the late seventies I left Trinidad to study visual arts at a university in Canada. When I returned home after the completion of my studies, the foreign wife of one of my father's patients was introduced to me by her in-laws, friends of my parents, as someone with whom I would have much in common. Elena was a lover of the arts; I was a painter. She was an Indophile and a student of Hinduism, I a Hindu of Indian ancestry. We were both passionate about nature and the outdoors: hiking, bird-watching, insect collecting.

Elena was a dark-haired, ruddy-coloured Spanish-Moroccan woman who could pass for tanned White, and she spoke little English. Before marrying her Trinidadian husband she had been a fashion model for a well-known European magazine. Though we were fast becoming friends, I was reluctant to be caught watching her directly. If my desire was suppressible in every other way, I knew that my eyes would betray me. What I found myself feeling for her, in a place like Trinidad, in a family like mine, like hers, was without question out of the question. In a jumble of Spanish and English and hand signs and laughter we would talk art and books and spirituality and nature, and I would keep my distance.

Elena was exactly the kind of woman my father was drawn to. She was stunningly beautiful and performed femininity eloquently, as if it were a craft. Her affectations were exaggerated without being excessive. The combination of her gentle manner, naive charm and on-the-edge couture attire was a perfected lure, yet her disposition, a kind of innocent arrogance, kept her admirers at a safe distance. I saw men get foolishly tongue-tied around her and caught other women observing her with envy.

One day Elena and I made a plan to visit at my parents' house. As it happened, every member of my busy family had an engagement elsewhere, and to my terror and surprise I found myself, for the first time ever, entirely alone with her. In the living room she sat on the couch; I made sure to sit in an armchair. The house was quiet and the air between us thick. In the heat of the day I could almost smell her skin. I contrived for us to walk in the garden, to look at the plants, for me to recite to her their botanical names and peculiarities. I told her that in the evening, when the sun drops into the sea and the heat subsides, *Beaumontia grandiflora* pumps and spreads its scent like a net over the evening. I offered her cuttings of *Hibiscus schizopetalus*, passing the com-

S h a n i   M o o t o o

mon velvety red ones and stopping at the prized hybrids:
orange ones with black centres, yellow ones with crimson
centres, my favourites. To point things out to me she would
touch my arm, pull me along momentarily by engaging one
of my fingers. When the sun became unbearable, sweat
beading like pearls along the wispy hairline at her temples,
we retreated to the library. A silence began to grow between
us. Our actions became deliberate and awkward. I took care
not to stand too close. As she drew a finger along the spines
of some large leather-bound books she asked, "You know
about us Spanish girls?"

I turned my back to her and, hoarse, said, "What's
there to know?"

"You don't know? We like girls." I couldn't respond. A
heat came over me. I turned around to find her standing
there, facing me. I was holding a book in both hands
between us. She looked down at the book, at my hands, and
said, "You have small hands. Not like mine. Let me see."

She held up one of hers, palm facing me. Putting the
book down I placed mine against it. Her hand was hot. My
breathing quickened and the room seemed to get dark, as if
the sun had ducked behind a cloud. Our fingers entwined.

She slowly pulled me by the hand toward her and she put her lips to mine. Her skin was damp, something primordial in her scent, or perhaps in my recognition of it. I pulled back and quickly unhinged my hand in fear and awe. Her face reddened and she withdrew immediately. Flushed, she began to apologize, but before she could finish her sentence I leaned forward and kissed her properly.

For the next year we kissed properly and improperly, exploring each other and inventing ways of being that were new to us both. Lacking models or mentors, we wrestled with what and who we were to each other, and like water finds its path we found ours. I became the focus of her femininity, which was no longer wily but had become raging and wild and demanding. In Elena's presence it was hopeless for me to bother with attempts to appear remotely female. While I had resisted girl-wear all my life, she brought out the boy in me. I became grander, larger than myself in order to contain her. I wore makeup less and had my hair cut short, in the androgynous fashion that was then hot in the U.S. and Britain but would never catch fire in Trinidad. We marvelled at and were terrified by the power and force of a passion that could only be expressed in secret.

S h a n i   M o o t o o

It was unusual for two women to seek each other out so intently and so frequently. Over time, it was evident in the glares my parents hurled my way that they suspected something, though I wonder if they even had a language for what that might have been. My father withdrew from me. It was not necessary for him to voice his profound disapproval and scorn, but I imagined he was also infuriated that his daughter had been given what he and so many other men had yearned for.

Elena and I talked often of running away together, although we both feared the scandal and the wrath that would follow. Much as I wanted to be with her, I did not want to lose my family or to hurt them. But this new self of mine was intoxicating. It was as if the old me had been a bud forever on the verge, and the new one was an opening out, a flowering A choice had to be made: a life of secrets or the freedom to realize my fullest potential. It was impossible after such glimpses of emancipation to return to being a bud. Within a year of meeting Elena, I left Trinidad, and her, and emigrated to British Columbia.

For a while I got involved with numerous women of the long wavy dark-brown hair, solid, confident variety.

Often they were married or had previously been straight. We satisfied some need in each other. I imagine theirs was the particular permission I afforded. Mine? A silent communiqué to my father, perhaps.

My recent novel, *Cereus Blooms at Night*, has outed me beyond any safe place. Not needing to hide has its rewards; when one is visible and takes pleasure in being seen, one no longer needs to use clothing as a signifier, insurance against mistaken identity. One doesn't have to perform the part, either. One's business is all out, in bright lights. Nowadays I feel less and less the need to dress like a boy. When I do, it is costume, performing butchness. It is play, not survival.

I used to wonder, and was sometimes asked, if I "became" lesbian because I was sexually abused as a child. Was it because I wanted to shake a fist at my father and avenge my mother? Because I wanted the freedom and power that my father and other men flaunt? Or did I simply come into the world with an eye for the girls? Content as I am these days, those questions and their answers no longer interest me. What does is the potential inherent in recognizing the finer details, the shapes and patterns of my desire.

Shani Mootoo

I am rivetted now by a woman who has none of the qualities that would attract my father. In fact, her quick intelligence, forthrightness, artsy fashion sense and belief that every moment is politically charged would no doubt repel him. That she slides seamlessly in and out of traditionally "male" or "female" behaviour allows me to do the same. We play opposites to each other, mirror each other, and our every interaction brings me an opportunity to discover new facets of myself. I am left with a wonderful giddiness and certainty. The monologue addressed to my father has ended.

Not too long ago, as my girlfriend pottered about the apartment we shared in New York City, she passed our bedroom and spotted me on the bed, reading. She glanced in, smiled, and continued on. Minutes later she returned with her camera and tentatively asked if I minded a candid shot. I remember well the moment of her asking, and of my impetuous consent.

It is a colour snapshot. A red brick wall covered with framed family photographs, her artwork and mine, and some quirky collectibles forms a vibrant backdrop to the captured domesticity. Up against the wall is a heavy wood-framed bed on which I recline entirely naked. Her two cats, one grey and one tiger-striped, loll atop the rumpled covers. Her dog, Lily, medium-sized and brindled, and mine, Frankie, a tricolour Shih Tzu, are sprawled face to face, sniffing each other on the floor beside the bed amidst an assortment of shoes, books, magazines and dog toys. I am looking at my photographer, relaxed and smiling, enjoying having this picture taken. I had never before per-mitted such an image to be made of me, but I recall the peacefulness and satisfaction I felt as the shutter clicked. I experienced in that moment what I had slowly uncovered over the years: there was nothing I needed to hide. My skin and all that it wrapped itself around was unequivocally mine, and finally I belonged to me.

ARRIVING
AT DESIRE

Dionne Brand

ARRIVING
AT DESIRE

I T IS ONLY NOW I recall, when recalling is all art, that the first book I read, falling into it like a fish falling into water, was a book about the Haitian revolution of 1791. It was owned by my uncle, a teacher, and it had no cover. The pages were thick and absorbent, their colour a yellowish cream from age, the ink still dark and pungent. The book had lain in the bottom drawer of the wardrobe for as long as I could remember, with a book on mathematics—geometry—and a Bible that was my grandmother's.

It was the same drawer where my grandmother kept stores of rice and sugar, syrup shine breads, just-in-case goods and, around Christmas, black cakes. She stored them under her good tablecloth, her good sheets and her good pillowcases. So the book was walked over by little red sugar ants; it was bored through by weevils. It was mapped by silverfish. It was thick with the humidity of rainy-season days and dry with the aridity of dry-season days. It had no spine, though it had a back. It had been sewn together, though the sewing was loose in some places, the thread almost rotted. It had been glued. The glue now caked in caramel-like flakes from the original binding.

I recall the title running over the top of each page: *The Black Napoleon*. I recall that the first letter of each chapter was larger than the rest of the words. I remember certain names—Toussaint, Henri Christophe, Dessalines . . . I cannot recall the author. I've never checked to see if such a book actually existed. I've never looked for or found that particular book again. I prefer to think of it still at the bottom of the wardrobe drawer, waiting for me to fall into its face.

The wardrobe was brown, the colour of mahogany. The bottom drawer was deep. It was heavy and it would

Dionne Brand

stick at times—a pillowcase caught in the groove, wood lice altering its tracks—requiring some skill to open it quietly. There was always a fine dust in the drawer, the work of colonies of insects moving their unseeable world to and fro. The book moved around from corner to corner too. I do not remember if it began with a first chapter. I suspect not. The front cover had long disappeared.

What made me fall into this book was likely some raid on my grandmother's cakes or sweet breads. I was probably trying to steal her Klim milk powder or the sugar she buried there, as if it were not the sole ambition of children to seek out secrets. She rotated her hiding places, of course, but the wardrobe could always be counted on because before my siblings and I ruined it there was a lock. And she kept the key in her bosom or under her pillow. My grandmother read the Bible from that drawer, putting her finger under each word then tiring, her eyes giving out or her grasp; she placed it in the recess at the head of her bed before falling asleep, some psalm dying on her lips. "The Lord is my rock, and my fortress, and my deliverer; my God, my strength in who I will trust; my buckler, and the horn of my salvation, and my high tower . . ." The psalm was a prohibition to our desire and a sign of her power, attached so intimately, so ardently to "the Lord." It was a psalm denoting her territory, the breadth of her command. But when she was asleep we forgot her power. Then the wardrobe drawer was a lure of table-cloth-covered cakes soaked in rum to keep them moist and crumbling shortbreads in tins from away, powdered milk and Ponds pink face powder, dates, chocolates melting to cherried centres in the heat, Andrew liver salts that frothed in the mouth, avocados left in brown paper to ripen. What led me to this book then were my senses, my sweet tooth, my hunger, my curiosity, the possibility of outsmarting my grandmother.

The geometry book I remember only as pages of drawings, signs and symbols with thick dense writing I could not follow, though I remember elaborate structures, a kind of inexplicable intelligence I knew I would never conquer but felt I ought to. The geometry book had lain in the drawer for years as companion to *The Black Napoleon*. But I never got close to it. I have always been bad at geometry.

I cannot recall the day I decided to read *The Black Napoleon*, but it must have been the day after my uncle said not to touch it. Then it became as irresistible as the other contents of the drawer. I opened the book, at first leaving the drawer open with the book lying inside, and began to read. Then I took it to my spot behind the house, then to my spot below the bed. The book filled me with sadness and courage. It burned my skin. I lay asleep on its open face under the bed. It was the book that took me away from the world, from the small intrigues of sugar and milk to the pleasure and desolation of words on a page.

For days I lived with the people I found there, hoping and urging and frightened and elated. The book was about the uprising led by Toussaint L'Ouverture against the French on Ste. Domingue. In it I met a history I was never taught. The history I had been taught began, "In 1492 Christopher Columbus discovered Santo Domingo ... With his three ships, the *Niña*, the *Pinta* and the *Santa María*, he discovered the New World." I had been given the first sighting of land by Cristóbal Colón as my beginnings. His eyes, his sight, his vindication, his proof, his discovered terrain: these were to be mine. All the moil and hurt proceeding from his view were to the good, evolutionary, a right and just casualty of modernity. Everything was missing from the middle of that story. Empire was at the end. So I had never met Toussaint

L'Ouverture until I saw him at the bottom of the wardrobe drawer with the cakes and sugar. Perhaps I also met there things I had never felt before. I did not know about slavery; I had never felt pain over it. In fact I had never felt pain except the kind of pain that children feel, immediate and transient; I had never seen—well, what can one see in eight years or so of living?—suffering. I did not yet know how the world took people like me. I did not know history. The book was a mirror and an ocean.

Dessalines was said in the pages of this book to have been voracious in battle, Toussaint a diplomat. When I was twenty-five or so, I would write in a poem, "Toussaint, I loved you as soon as I saw you on that page." I loved his faith, though it betrayed him. But Dessalines' ardour never would. I loved his ferocity. The poem ended, "Dessalines, Dessalines, you were right . . ." This book I had found inhabited me with its terror and revolution. It was the first "big" book I would read to its end. When I was finished, I was made. I had lost innocence and acquired knowledge. I had lost the idea that desire was plain.

Edouard Glissant, the Martiniquan critic, says that "History is destined to be pleasure or distress." For me *The*

Black Napoleon was both. I recall the passion I felt for those people fighting the French. I recognized them. I was them. I remember my small chest, my grandmother called it a bird's chest, wracked with apprehension over the outcome. I would continue to hunt down sugar and milk and black fruitcake and cream wafers, certainly, but *The Black Napoleon* and falling into the face of a book were now entwined in my sensual knowledge. I read the book over and over again, returning to passages. To Toussaint and Dessalines.

The second book I recall, as one only recalls significance, and recollection is happenstance (things that leave sufficient impression to break the surface of thousands of thoughts and experiences) and then again selection, the second book I recall is D. H. Lawrence's *Lady Chatterley's Lover*. This book began as a rumour at twelve or thirteen, a rumour in a girls' high school about a forbidden book. Forbidden because there were "good" parts. When we got hold of the book it was all we could do to keep it hidden from the teachers. So amazing and unvarnished were its descriptions that our own language became secretive, even unspoken. I have not read it since. The truth is, I remember only a gardener (gamekeeper? gatekeeper?), a lady, a kind of anxiety, a kind of exquisite agony I looked forward to having some day. The book had a red cover. It was pored over and crushed. The pages with the good stuff were creased. I remember reading quickly. I remember too a feeling of being older, having read it, worldly. As if I had been let into another skin, a woman's, a man's, a country's. But I also felt burdened, as if I knew something that I should not, something that had changed me into the girl who had read *Lady Chatterley's Lover*, different from the girl who had not read it a moment ago. So ravishing were the book's contents that I think each of us only had the chance to read certain paragraphs hastily. Perhaps different paragraphs, perhaps different stresses for the words of particular sentences. We read quickly, looking up after every line to see if we were in danger of being found out. We could not betray each other, or we would lose the possibility of ever knowing the good parts. We had only the one book. We covered it in brown paper, I think, as my grandmother had covered the avocados, to ripen. We rationed it, keeping only so many paragraphs apiece, so many lines. I read holding my breath, the narrative interpolated into the humid air of a going-home-after-school after-

Dionne   Brand

noon. A not-watching-where-you-are-going, stumbling, perhaps falling afternoon.

I like to think of us now, eight or so women then girls, each in a different part of the world, each in possession of a different paragraph of *Lady Chatterley's Lover*, a different line now perhaps interrupted, intercut by how we have chosen to live our lives. I do not know who among us iden-tified with the lady and who with the gamekeeper. The book's gendering could not have been seamless. No book's gendering can be, ultimately, since a book asks us to embody, which at once takes us across borders of all kinds. Or does it dispel borders altogether? Anyway, some of us were him and some of us were her. She seemed light, lim-nal; he seemed dark, brooding consciousness. This para-digm of the canon was a conflict for us. We were she *and* he—female and darkly brooding. Both the possibilities and the constraints of enactment existed within the borderless territory of the book. We were beckoned by some famil-iarity with her in us, we were willing, eager, to be her. Yet at the same moment we saw in ourselves the "not-her"; she was an ideal of a society which stood in powerful relation to ours. The conversation going on in the book was about culture, class, technology and sexuality. It was the same conversation going on in our lives and it was the conversation going on between the place where the book lived and the place where we lived. This conflict was not fully charged in us yet. So we wanted to be her, we wanted to be them, we wanted to be there. Yet we recognized the cleavage, the primitive in his cottage at the bottom of the garden, modernity attracted and repelled by him. We were him. We, on an island at the bottom of the New World, we too were representations of the primitive.

The book had begun outside of the book, in the rumour. We had begun outside of the book also, the colonial conscious, the female conscious. When we entered the book, entering for the purposes of identifying and enacting, we were flung apart. We disintegrated, we abstracted. We emerged having reconstructed the novel into a more complex, more fluid sense of desire.

"Literature . . . quarries itself in us," Edouard Glissant says, "as a consciousness." *The Black Napoleon* and *Lady Chatterley's Lover* gave me a refractory hunger. Their register and compass led me to all the books that followed.

My uncle let me keep *The Black Napoleon*. It became my book. I do not recall sharing it with my sisters or my cousins or my friends. That time I tried to run away from home at fourteen I tied it around with a belt along with the rest of my books, going I don't know where. No clothes, no shoes, just books and three dollars. I could not take *Lady Chatterley's Lover*; I did not have it all. I only had a few lines shared with a few girls.

Books leave gestures in the body, a certain way of moving, of turning, a certain closing of the eyes, a way of leaving, hesitations. Books leave certain sounds, a certain pacing; mostly they leave the elusive, which is all the story. They leave much more than the words. Words can be thrown together. It is their order, and when they catch you—their time. These first two books shaped me. And I suspect that I have been writing these two books ever since, recalling and reimagining them. I had been seduced by them. The fact is I remember them only in my body. I cannot quote a single line from them, and I have not ever felt the need to return to them physically, though I know that I always return to them as I write. The emotions they spoke of were contradictory to what one might simplistically call desire. But desire is disclosed as a complex. There is a range of experience within the space which is called desire. Toussaint and Dessalines embodied faith and ferocity, different constructs which amplified my sense of desire. The lady and the gamekeeper embodied dissonances of the physical body, the racial body and the gendered body. The canonical locations of light and dark, male, female, master, slave were broken or interrupted in both books. Desire's province widened to the flying pieces, their occasional collection into a movement or a colour or a sigh, ever shifting, ever reimagined.

Writing is an act of desire, as is reading. Why does someone enclose a set of apprehensions within a book? Why does someone else open that book, if not in the act of wanting to be wanted, to be understood, to be seen, to be loved?

And desire is also an act of reading, of translation. The poet Joy Harjo writes, "Nearly everyone had left that bar in the middle of winter except the / hardcore. It was the coldest night of the year, every place shut down, but / not us. Of course we noticed when she came in. We were Indian ruins. She / was the end of beauty."

Desire too is the discovery of beauty as miraculous. Desire in the face of ruin. How in these lines there is such wreckage and that too is beauty, how in those lines there is such clear-eyed dread, such deeply mocking knowledge, and that too is desire. How those lines read beauty and desire into any given night. In any place, trailer park waste-land, rural rum shop, shebeen, sports bar, speakeasy, piss- and beer-reeking dive, beauty walks in. On any given night, even with history against you in any hardscrabble place, beauty walks in. The ruin of history visited on a peo-ple does not wipe out the steadfastness of beauty. Not a naive beauty, but a hard one. Beauty, it seems, is constantly made. It is both fortunate and unfortunate. Surprising.

For some, to find beauty is to search through ruins. For some of us beauty must be made over and over again out of the sometimes fragile, the sometimes dangerous. To write is to be involved in this act of translation, of succumbing to this fragility and danger, of leaning into another body's idiom. Some years ago a young man surely on his own way to ruin stepped into the street on a square in Amsterdam, the night just approaching. I watched him from a distance. His figure was in anguish and discomfort; it jangled, it wanted to be and not to be in the square. He was in a kind of despair I have never experienced and experienced then only through his drifting into the street. My despair is private, but his was public and private all at once. His drifting into the street, his slight hesitation—this was beauty. I saw that young man drop into the square like a drop of water into an ocean. That is, I saw his body, his back half-turned toward me, his right leg hovering before stepping off the curb. My eyes followed his yellow-clad body—or it seemed to be yellow in that dark street. The square had a way of darkening with secrets so the light was yellow, his figure was yellow. That was beauty, his anguish was beauty; his leg stopping, his face whipping round in search of someone, yet his disinterest somehow in people, the glaze over his eyes, yet their sharpness in seeking out the thing, the someone he was after, all was beauty. He was someone in his own gesture, the thing that writers envy. This gesture was clever and cold, edgy, and belonged to him. To desire then, to read and translate, may also be to envy, to want to become. What is it that I wanted to pour myself into, his grief, his cold sweat, his life uncertain of its next step? And I wanted to do it only for the moment it took to feel its tex-

Dionne Brand

ture, and then to run back quickly to my uncomplicated hotel room and my as yet uncomplicated page. To desire may also be to complicate.

I wanted to say something else about desire. I really do not know what it is. I experience something which, sometimes, if I pull it apart, I cannot make reason of. The word seems to me to fall apart under the pull and drag of its commodified shapes, under the weight of our artifice and our conceit. It is sometimes impossible to tell what is real from what is manufactured. We live in a world filled with mass-produced images of desire. Desire clings to widgets, chairs, fridges, cars, perfumes, shoes, jackets, golf clubs, basketballs, telephones, water, soap powder, houses, neighbourhoods, even god. It clings to the faces of television sets and movie screens. It is glaciered in assigned objects, it is petrified in clichéd gestures. Their repetition is tedious, the look and sound of them tedious. We become the repetition despite our best efforts. We become numb. And though against the impressive strength of this I cannot hope to say all that desire might be, I wanted to talk about it not as it is sold but as one collects it, piece by piece, proceeding through a life. I wanted to say that life, if we are lucky, is a collection of aesthetic experiences, as it is a collection of practical experiences, which if we are lucky we make a sense of. Making sense may be what desire is. Or putting the senses back together.

EROS

Carol Shields

EROS

shields

ANN WENT TO A PARTY one night where the dinner conversation drifted toward the subject of sexuality. How does the sexual self get sparked into life? And when do we suspect its shared presence?

The man sitting next to Ann at the table spoke authoritatively on the subject. The sexual act, he said, requires a verbal gloss these days. Other creatures—lesser creatures, he meant—act out their sexuality instinctively, but human beings have evolved to the point where they must second-guess all natural feelings. A case of cultural over-refinement. It can happen that people, so busy learning mathematics or looking after their hair, simply don't "get it" on their own, and then they need a sort of interpretive guide like those types who take you on tours around hydraulic dams or conduct wildflower walks. "These days explication is required," he said, "in order to sanction the commands of the blood."

Ann disagreed with this man and said so. His name was Alex, and she'd been told he was a well-respected maker of mediaeval instruments with a studio in a converted warehouse not far from where she lives. She suspected he had been invited for her sake—it happened all the time, the well-intentioned matchmaking of her coupled friends. And so here they were, a single man, a divorced woman, the two of them seated next to each other, at the long, festive dinner table. Ann thought Alex's phrase "commands of the blood" was silly and old-fashioned, like certain kinds of poetry she remembered from school.

"Which is why," Alex continued, "we have had to develop the awful institution of the birds-and-bees talk between parents and children. Otherwise new generations

Carol Shields

could miss the whole thing, the mechanics, as it were, of what is required."

"That seems impossible," someone across the table said. "People don't grow to adulthood without knowing they're sexual animals."

Alex was adamant. He leaned his long arm forward so that the hairs on the back of his gesticulating hand were whitened by the twin circles of candlelight. "Individual children feel sexual urges, of course, but they don't necessarily know that other people do."

"You only have to turn on the TV—"

"And in prime time too!"

"—the new play at the Playhouse, I mean, talk about graphic—"

"Couldn't be more explicit."

"When I asked my mother about sex, she just wrung her hands and said, 'Don't you already know!' "

"More people than we think are locked in a circle of innocence," Alex said, nodding in a way that Ann thought was pretentious. "They resist. They block."

"All they have to do is read the newspaper."

"—spells out the whole whammy."

"Desire," said the woman whose dinner party it was. She stared deeply into her glass of red wine and said it again. "Desire."

The subject turned to Victorian brides who went to their marriage beds uninformed, how shocking that must have been, how perverse they must have found their husbands' expectations. *Now, my precious love, there is something I'm going to have to poke between your legs, but I promise to be gentle . . .*

"Maybe it did happen occasionally," Ann said, "but only someone terribly stupid could arrive at marriage age without adding up the perfectly obvious evidence all around them."

"You mean," someone said, "observing farm animals and the like?"

"Well, yes. And common everyday romance, which has always been out in the open. Kissing, touching. Erotic glances. You have to know something's going on, that men and women have more happening between them than polite conversation and domestic convenience."

"Some people aren't particularly observant," Alex said, which suggested to Ann that he might be one of those people. "And some people aren't good at connecting the dots even when they see them."

Carol Shields

A woman called Nancy Doyen mentioned a story she'd read in an American newspaper. An Alabama couple had been married for a period of three years, at which time they visited a doctor, wondering why they had not been blessed with a baby. The doctor asked a few tactful questions, and soon established the fact that the couple had not had sexual relations. They had believed that sharing a bed—sleeping together—was all that was required.

"My point exactly!" Alex cried out. His voice was excited.

Ann gave him a long sideways look. He was the only man at the table who was not wearing a jacket and tie. Instead he wore a soft-looking woollen sweater in a deep shade of blue. Indigo, she supposed it would be called. The knit was particularly small and smooth for a man's sweater, and Ann reached forward and placed her hand lightly on the ribbing that formed the sweater's cuff. She had the idea that she must somehow restrain this person from making a fool of himself. He was looking into the candlelight with a Zenlike concentration, and Ann knew how, after a certain amount of wine, Zen talk leads straight to embarrassment.

He continued, though, her hand still resting on his wrist, to talk about the complicated notion of human sexuality, its secret nature and hidden surprises, its unlikelihood, in fact. As he talked he covered Ann's hand with his own, and then with one slow, almost absent-minded gesture he swept her hand into the shadows of his lap. She could feel the rough linen of the table napkin, then the abrupt soft corduroy of his trousers. She flexed her fingers, an involuntary movement, and a moment later found her hand resting against human flesh, the testicles laughably loose in their envelope of fine skin, and a penis, flaccid and small, curled up like a blind animal. Meat and two veg was how she and her girlfriends once described this part of the male body.

At first she thought she might laugh, and then she decided she might faint. She had never fainted in all her life, but this could be the moment. No one would blame her, especially those who knew about her recent surgery and chemo treatments.

Couldn't the others at the table hear the gasp gathering in her throat? She made a motion to pull her hand away from Alex's lap, but he pressed his fingers more firmly on

Carol Shields

hers. The thought came to her that these were the same fingers that constructed intricate lutes and lyres and handled small, probably beautiful tools. Her consciousness seemed to divide and to divide again, and then soften. She moved her fingers slightly, playfully, seeing what experiments she might invent. Even so small a movement had the effect of sucking the air out of the room, though no one seemed to notice.

"Desire," the hostess said once again. She probed her salad greens gently, then put down her fork and peered around the table of guests, a long visual arc of inquiry, of solicitude. Her wine glass was empty. Her look was loving and also proprietorial. She appeared pleased with every single one of them.

When Ann was four years old she was taken to stay for a few days with a married cousin who lived in the country. She has no idea how the arrangement came about. What could it have meant—a gesture of hospitality extended to a very young child? She does remember that she considered the visit a thrilling adventure.

Her cousin Sandra was a young woman, barely twenty,

with a musical laugh and curls all over her head. She lived in a small brown house on an acre of land with her young husband, Gerald, and a tiny baby, Merry-Ann. There was about these arrangements the sense of a doll family afloat in a toy landscape, and this should have constituted a paradise for little Ann, whose own parents seemed immensely old and sombre and without movement in their lives.

She was allowed to push Merry-Ann in her carriage, first covering her with a crocheted blanket and tucking in the edges. She was permitted to stand on a kitchen chair and mash potatoes with Cousin Sandra's wooden masher. When Sandra and Gerald kissed, as they often did, Ann had the feeling of being inside the pages of a beautiful pop-up book with defined edges and dimensions and sudden, swallowed surprises and jokes.

Nevertheless, within a few days, three or four at the most, she grew anxious and miserable. She complained to her cousin of an earache, but the cousin identified the malady for what it was: severe homesickness. Her small suitcase was packed, and she was driven home.

She remembers that she was carried through the doorway of her own house—in whose arms she can never quite

Carol Shields

recall—and that she found the neutral, neglected rooms extraordinarily altered. In fact, only a few items had been changed. A leaf had been taken out of the breakfast table, and this smaller squarish table was now positioned at an angle under the window. Instead of the usual tan placemats there was a brightly flowered cloth, one Ann had never seen, and this too was placed at an angle. The scene was as jaunty and brave as a Rinso ad. Bright sunlight struck the edges of the plates and cups so that she had the sense of looking into a bowl of brilliant confetti, there were so many particles of colour dancing before her eyes.

This transformation had occurred in the short time she'd been away. It seemed impossible.

And even more impossible was the idea that her parents had been here all along. They had not been frozen in time or whisked out of sight. They had been alive, busily transforming the unalterable everyday surfaces, and here was the evidence. In her absence they had prevailed. They possessed, it seemed clear, an existence of their own.

And there was something else that folded and filled the air. Something disturbing, vivid. It had no taste or noise to it, but it bulked in the space between her aproned mother and her father with his loosened necktie and rolled-up sleeves. "It" was a charged force, not that she could have described it as such, from which she herself was excluded, and it connected as through an underground passage with Cousin Sandra and Gerald kissing by the kitchen window, their mouths so teasing against each other, and yet so purposeful.

But that was all right. She liked it that way, and even if she didn't, she understood that this was the way things were and had, in fact, always been.

Yes, there was a thickening in the air, the spiked ether of unanswered questions.

But this was nothing new. Huge patches of mystery existed everywhere. How, for instance, to explain the halo around the head of the baby Jesus? How did the voices get into the radio? That time when two neighbourhood dogs got stuck together: how could such an unlikely thing happen?

Ann, age seven, was caught at school holding a note that was being passed from desk to desk. The teacher, Miss Sellers, snatched it away and quickly scanned its contents. "I'm surprised at you, Ann," she said. "I'm very, very disappointed."

The note said: "Nelly, put your belly up to mine and wiggle your behind."

Ann was asked to stay in from recess until she had copied ten lines on a piece of paper: "I will not pass notes again." Later, deeply shamed and making her way out to the playground, she saw Miss Sellers in the stairwell. She was showing the note to two other teachers and they were laughing their heads off.

Aunt Alma and Uncle Ross came to visit every summer, and this visit was greatly anticipated, especially by Ann's mother. Aunt Alma was her favourite sister and the most beautiful. She wore daringly cut cotton dresses she made herself and was lively in her manner, spilling gossip and laughter. She knew how to "go at a tear," ripping through the household tasks, the beds, the dishes, so that she and Ann's mother could head off for a day of shopping or out to lunch at a place called the Spinning Wheel. Sometimes, when Aunt Alma thought Ann was out of earshot, she told slightly off-colour jokes—but with a sense of wonderment in her voice, as though she herself with her elegant posture and thick coiled hair stood just outside the oxygen of these jokes, slightly bewildered rather than amused by the small, rough ironies of human bodies and the language that attended them.

Uncle Ross was tall, thin and solemn. He spent the vacation days seated in a porch chair and going through a stack of *Reader's Digests* he'd brought along. There was no time to read during the working year, he explained; he was kept so busy at the insurance company.

One evening at the dinner table Uncle Ross paused before taking his place next to Aunt Alma. It happened to be a particularly hot day, and Aunt Alma was wearing a backless sundress. He bent and kissed the back of her neck, a slow and courtly kiss, unhurried, serious and private— never mind that the whole family was present and about to dig into their roast beef hash.

This kissed part of Aunt Alma's neck was called the nape, which was something Ann didn't know at the time.

Ann, who must have been seven or eight years old, watched the kiss from across the table, and it seemed to her the kiss fell on her neck too, on that same shivery spot.

She felt her whole body stiffen into a kind of pleasurable yawn that went on and on. So this was it. Now she knew.

Ann at fourteen spent hours at her desk practicing an elegant backhand, which she believed would move her life forward. Her daily life was fuzzy, composed of what felt like carpet lint and dust, when what she wanted was clarity, poignancy. She memorized a love sonnet by Edna St. Vincent Millay, and she and her friend Lorna recited it in low moony tones, making fun of the words and of their own elocutionary efforts. She stared at the khaki pants of the boys in her class and wondered what was there packed into the crotch and how it felt. Some boys she didn't know stopped her on her way home from school and poked a tree branch between her legs, which frightened her and puzzled her too, so that she broke away and ran all the way to her house. She cried at the movies; in fact, she only liked those movies that made her cry; her tears were beautiful to her, so clear, fast-flowing and willing, yet so detached from her consciousness that she could watch them and mock them and snort at how foolish they were and how they betrayed her. At a New Year's Eve party a boy kissed her; it was part of a game, something he was obliged to do by the game's rules, but nevertheless she relived the moment at least once each day as though it were a piece of high drama, the softness of his lips and the giggling, eager embarrassment he'd shown. All these unsorted events accumulated in the same pocket of her brain, breathing with their own warm set of lungs. She read *Lady Chatterley's Lover*, and what shocked her most was that she found the book under a chair in her mother's bedroom.

Her mother knew; that was the terrible part. Her father knew too, he would have to know if her mother knew. Everyone knew this awful secret which was everywhere suggested but which for Ann lay, still, a quarter-inch out of reach. Even Bob Hope on the radio knew; you could tell by the way he talked about blondes and brunettes and redheads. Oh, he knew.

"Don't ever let a boy touch your knee," Ann's mother told her. "It happened to me once when I was your age, but I knew that one thing could lead to another."

"A climax is like a sneeze," one of Ann's girlfriends said. "And you know how much everyone loves to sneeze."

Carol Shields

"Boys love it if you put your finger in their ear. Not too hard, though. Just a tickle."

"The Tantric secrets," said an article Ann read in *Esquire* magazine, "can be easily mastered in a three-day course given on the shores of the beautiful Finger Lakes."

"I hope he never touched you," Ann's father said about Uncle Ross. "You'd tell us, wouldn't you, if he touched you."

High up on her inner thigh. That's where Ann touched herself. Making a little circle with her thumb.

"Sex and death. They live in the same breath, can't you feel that?" This from an English professor who detained Ann after class one day in order to discuss her essay on Byron.

"Be a nun and you get none," said an actress in a play Ann attended. The woman pronounced it loudly from centre stage, full of sly winks and meaningful shrugs.

"The body is a temple. Keep that temple sanctified for the man you are going to spend your life with. On the other hand, it's usually better if the man has had a little prior experience."

Molly Bloom. Yes, she said, yes, she said, yes. Something like that.

Ann married Benjamin. She had both her breasts in those days, and Benjamin adored those breasts. "You'd think they'd squeak when the nipple goes up," he said with wonder. He toyed with them, sucked them, gnawed gently at the tender breast skin, saying, "Grrrrr." The brown colour of the twin aureoles astonished him, though. He had expected pink, like in a painting. Ann wondered if the brownness frightened him slightly.

They had a wedding night, the kind of wedding night no one gets any more. Before that night there had been long, luscious sessions of kissing, accompanied by a carefully programmed fumbling with each other's bodies: nothing below the waist, nothing under the clothes allowed, but nevertheless it was rapturous, those wet deep kisses and shy touches on her sweatered breasts.

Now here, suddenly, was Ann in a white silk nightgown with a lace yoke. Then the nightgown came quickly off, which seemed a shame considering its cost. Now his whole body was against hers; head to toe their warm young skin was in contact. This was the best part. The rest of the business hurt, and left a sticky, bloody puddle on the

Carol Shields

bedsheet, which worried Ann, how the hotel staff probably had to deal with such messes all the time.

She and Benjamin had read the marriage manual their minister had given them, and in the chapter titled "Afterwards," the author had described a feeling of vague melancholy which often visits couples after a session of satisfying sex. There was a reason for this, something chemical, the hormones plunging to the baseline flatness of everyday life, a necessary return to the reality that sustains us.

And, yes, Ann remembered that wedding night plunge. Her whole body trembled with the sadness of it, and Benjamin, mistaking the trembling for orgasm, was proud, and then exhilarated, and then almost immediately ready to go again. "Grrrrr," he said against her chest wall.

Things got better, of course. Then they got worse. Then they dramatically dwindled. There were violent quarrels in the early years that made Ann think of cloth tearing behind her eyes, and reconciliations so tender that even today her throat fills with tears when she recalls them. Sex was either a healing or an exercise in blame. Once she made the mistake of telling Benjamin that she found something faintly hilarious about sex, about how a man's penis suddenly blew up and wanted to stick itself in a woman's vagina; it was so ungainly, such a curious and clumsy human mechanism. He had taken this confidence badly. He liked to think of sex as a beautiful form of communion, he said, but Ann knows that he would not find her beautiful at this moment, with her battleground of a chest, that slicing breast scar and the curious new cords of hard tissue that join her shoulder and arm. Alex, sitting next to her at a dinner table, her thumb and forefinger on his penis, will not find it beautiful either, never mind the cheerful advice from the cancer booklets about the return of the libido and new forms of touching and holding.

Benjamin's shame, his promises, his failures, his ardour, his indecision—these formed the swampy terrain which Ann learned more or less to navigate, understanding that any minute the ground was likely to give way, but feeling at the same time stronger, and more certain about what she wanted. "I want you out," she finally said after one particularly bitter betrayal, and then, a week later, changed her mind.

They went to Paris to patch things up.

Carol Shields

Their hotel was located on a quiet street in the Marais and faced onto a private park where Parisians walked their dogs in the early mornings. Most of the other buildings in the neighbourhood were built of a dull basement-coloured stone, but the hotel where Ann and Benjamin stayed was, rather curiously, constructed of a soft, rosy, unParisian brick. Like many hotels, it wound its way around a rectangular air shaft so that each room looked directly into the windows of the other rooms. There was a small garden at the bottom and a few lines of laundry, still in the still air.

The hotel was classified as a luxury accommodation, but it seemed during the week they were there to be undergoing a form of entropy. The air conditioning failed. The fax connection to the outside world failed. The extraordinarily heavy curtain on Ann's and Benjamin's window fell to the floor, brass rod and all, and it took the two of them to carry it out to the corridor.

On the last day, after a breakfast of coffee and croissants, the elevator broke down. ("We do apologize, Madame, but it is only five flights, just think of the guests on the top floors.") She and Benjamin climbed the stairs and entered their room. The faint and not unpleasant smell of cigar smoke greeted them, smoke that must have drifted across the air shaft from another room.

Benjamin lay on the bed, his eyes closed, and Ann settled in a chair by the open window, spreading her newspaper in front of her. She loved to read *Le Monde* when she came to France; its linguistic turns seemed a sort of crossword puzzle, and each time she managed to translate a sentence she congratulated herself.

Church bells rang out from a distance, reminding her that it was a Sunday morning. Traffic sounds rose from the street. A dog was barking, probably from the park across the street. Then she heard something else: a woman's strong orgasmic cry coming from one of the open windows of the hotel.

The innocence of it was what moved her first, the stunning lack of restraint. The music of the woman's moan was immediately recognizable to Ann, this half-singing, half-weeping, wordless release that seemed to block out all of Paris, all of the hexagon of France with its borders and seacoast and muted overhead sky.

Benjamin's eyes were suddenly open. He was smiling at her, and she was smiling back. Then they were out of their clothes—this happened in an instant—and into each other's arms. His skin felt exactly right to her that day, its silver flecks and familiar imperfections. As they moved together on the hard French bed the rhythm of their bodies took them over, in tune for once, and it seemed to Ann that the red bricks of their hotel were melting into a pool of sensuality. She had never understood that curious, overweighted word *desire*, she had scoffed at that word, but this must be it, this force that funnelled through the open air, travelling through the porous masonry and entering her veins.

Everything, it seemed, could be forgiven and mended now. She imagined that each room on the air shaft was similarly transformed, that men and women were coming together ecstatically as she and Benjamin were doing and that the combined sounds they made formed an erotic random choir, whose luminous, unmoored music was spreading skyward over the city. This was all they ever needed for such perfect happiness, this exquisite permission, a stranger's morning cry.

Of course it didn't last, how could it?

But she hangs on to the moment in these difficult days,

even at this dinner table with her hand still in the lap of a man named Alex, whom she scarcely knows or even likes. She is part of the blissful and awakened world. Yes, this is what she must hang on to.

ABOUT THE CONTRIBUTORS

DIONNE BRAND is renowned as a poet, novelist and essayist. Her most recent collection of poetry, *Land to Light On*, won both the Governor General's Award and the Trillium Award in 1997. She is the author of two highly acclaimed novels, *In Another Place, Not Here* and *At the Full and Change of the Moon*.

BONNIE BURNARD's collection of stories *Women of Influence* (Coteau Books) received the Commonwealth Best First Book Award in 1989. A second collection, *Casino and Other Stories* (Phyllis Bruce/HarperCollins), received the Saskatchewan Book of the Year Award and was shortlisted for the Giller Prize. In 1995, Bonnie Burnard was honoured with the Marian Engel Award. Her novel *A Good House* was published in 1999 by Harper Flamingo.

LORNA CROZIER's poetry has received numerous national awards, including the Governor General's Award and two Pat Lowther Awards for the best book of poetry by a Canadian woman. Her essays, as well as her poetry, have been published widely in magazines and anthologies. Lorna Crozier presently teaches at the University of Victoria in British Columbia. Her tenth book of poetry, *What the Living Won't Let Go*, was published in 1999.

EVELYN LAU is the author of *Runaway: Diary of a Street Kid* (HarperCollins, 1989), *Fresh Girls and Other Stories* (Harper Collins, 1993), *Other Women* (Random House, 1995) and *Choose Me* (Doubleday, 1999), as well as three collections of poetry: *You Are Not Who You Claim*, *Oedipal Dreams* and *In the House of Slaves*. She is presently at work on a collection of essays.

SHANI MOOTOO was born in Ireland and grew up in Trinidad. A filmmaker and visual artist, she has written and directed several videos, and her paintings and photo-based works have been exhibited internationally. She is the author of *Out on Main Street*, a collection of short stories, and a novel, *Cereus Blooms at Night*, which was selected as a New England Booksellers Association's Discovery Title and was nominated for the Giller Prize, the Ethel Wilson Fiction Prize and the Chapters/*Books in Canada* First Novel Award. She currently makes her home in British Columbia.

SUSAN MUSGRAVE has published over twenty books, her most recent being *Things That Keep and Do Not Change*, a collection of poetry (McClelland and Stewart, 1999). A chapter from her recently completed novel, *Cargo of Orchids*, was published in *Fever: Sensual Stories by Women Writers*, edited by Michelle Slung (Harcourt Brace, 1994), and in *Best American Erotica, 1995*, edited by Susie Bright (Simon & Schuster). She and her husband, Stephen Reid, were the subjects of a recent CBC *Life and Times* documentary, "The Poet and the Bandit."

CAROL SHIELDS is the award-winning author of numerous novels, plays and story collections. Her 1993 novel *The Stone Diaries* won the Pulitzer Prize for Fiction, the Governor General's Award and the U.S. National Book Critics Circle Award, and was shortlisted for Britain's prestigious Booker Prize. Her most recent book, *Larry's Party*, won the 1997 Orange Prize for Fiction. Carol Shields lives with her husband in Winnipeg, where she is chancellor of the University of Winnipeg.

ACKNOWLEDGEMENTS

I WANT TO THANK Barbara Pulling of Douglas & McIntyre for inviting me to be the editor of this book, and I want to praise her amazingly sharp ear and eye. I've learned a lot from working with her. There's no editor with more perspicacity and insight. I also want to thank the six other writers who grace this book. All were enthusiastic about the project from the start. Reading and responding to their essays has been a delight. Finally, I'd like to express my appreciation for the advice and support of Patrick Lane, who is always with me in my life and words.

—L.C.

Excerpts from or references to the following sources are gratefully acknowledged. Epigraph: "A Breakfast for Barbarians" from *The Selected Poetry of Gwendolyn MacEwen, Volume 1: The Early Years*, edited by Margaret Atwood and Barry Callaghan (Toronto: Exile Editions, 1993). "Changing into Fire": Excerpt from "Some Sayings of the Desert Fathers" from *The Wisdom of the Desert*, translated by Thomas Merton (New York: New Directions, 1970); Excerpt from "Untitled" from *Interstices of Night* by Terrence Heath (Winnipeg: Turnstone Press, 1979) is used with the kind permission of the author. "Arriving at Desire": *Caribbean Discourse: Selected Essays* by Eduoard Glissant, translated by J. Michael Dash (Charlotteville, North Carolina: University Press of Virginia, 1989); Excerpt of "Deer Dancer" from *In Mad Love and War* © 1990 by Joy Harjo, Wesleyan University Press, by permission of the University Press of New England.

A c k n o w l e d g e m e n t s